ASPECTS
of PSYCHOLOGY

PERSPECTIVES
in PSYCHOLOGY

ASPECTS
of PSYCHOLOGY
PERSPECTIVES
in PSYCHOLOGY

RICHARD GROSS & ROB MCILVEEN

Hodder & Stoughton

A MEMBER OF THE HODDER HEADLINE GROUP

Dedication

To all students of Psychology: past, present and future

British Library Cataloguing in Publication Data
A catalogue record for this title is available from the British Library

ISBN 0 340 75347 1

First published 1999
Impression number   10 9 8 7 6 5 4 3 2 1
Year   2003 2002 2001 2000 1999

Typeset by GreenGate Publishing Services, Tonbridge, Kent.
Printed and bound in Great Britain for Hodder and Stoughton Educational, a division of Hodder Headline plc, 338 Euston Road, London NW1 3BH, by Cox & Wyman

CONTENTS

Preface   vii

Acknowledgements   viii

**1 An introduction to psychology and its
   approaches**   1
Introduction and overview; What is psychology?;
Classifying the work of psychologists; Major
theoretical approaches in psychology; Conclusions;
Summary

**2 The nature of the person in
   psychology: free will and
   determinism, and reductionism**   37
Introduction and overview; Free will and
determinism; Reductionism; Conclusions;
Summary

3 Controversial applications   63
Introduction and overview; Social influence,
behaviour change and ethics; Psychology,
propaganda and warfare; Advertising; Psychometric
testing; Conclusions; Summary

4 Psychology as a science   87
Introduction and overview; Some philosophical
roots of science and psychology; What do we mean
by 'science'?; Is it appropriate to study human
behaviour using scientific methods?; Conclusions;
Summary

**5 Bias in psychological theory
   and research**   117
Introduction and overview; Gender bias: feminist
psychology, sexism and androcentrism; Culture bias;
Conclusions; Summary

6 Ethical issues in psychology   **139**
Introduction and overview; Codes of conduct and
ethical guidelines; Psychologists as
scientists/investigators; Human participants; Non-
human subjects; Psychologists as practitioners;
Conclusions; Summary

References   **175**

Index   **185**

PREFACE

The *Aspects of Psychology* series aims to provide a short and concise, but detailed and highly accessible, account of selected areas of psychological theory and research.

Perspectives in Psychology consists of six chapters. Chapter 1 provides an introduction to Psychology and its major theoretical approaches. Chapter 2 discusses two major philosophical issues relating to the nature of the person in Psychology: free will and determinism, and reductionism. Chapter 3 considers controversial applications of psychological theory and research, including propaganda, advertising and pychometric testing. In Chapter 4, we discuss Psychology as a science, and in Chapter 5, the focus is on gender and culture bias in psychological theory and research. Finally, in Chapter 6, ethical issues are discussed as they arise in research with both humans and non-humans, as well as in applied psychology.

For the purposes of revision, we have included detailed summaries of the material presented in each chapter. Instead of a separate glossary, for easy reference the Index contains page numbers in **bold** which refer to definitions and main explanations of particular concepts. Chapters 2–6 also include exercises designed to help you draw on (and revise) your knowledge of the syllabus as a whole.

ACKNOWLEDGEMENTS

We would like to thank Dave Mackin, Anna Churchman and Denise Stewart at GreenGate Publishing for their swift and efficient preparation of the text. Thanks also to Greig Aitken at Hodder for all his hard work in coordinating this project (we hope it's the first of many!), and to Tim Gregson-Williams for his usual help and support.

Picture Credits

The publishers would like to thank the following for permission to reproduce photographs and other illustrations in this book:

p.8 (Fig 1.2), Corbis-Bettman; p.18 (Fig 1.4), Corbis-Bettman; p.23 (Fig 1.5), Corbis-Bettman; p.25 (Fig 1.6a,c,d), Corbis-Bettman; (Fig 1.6b), Olive Pearce/Robert Hunt Library; p.27 (Fig 1.7), Times Newspapers Ltd, London; p.29 (Fig 1.8), Corbis-Bettman; p.30 (Fig 1.9), Corbis-Bettman; p.71 (Box 3.3), from M Gilbert, (1986) *The Holocaust: The Jewish Tragedy*. Harper Collins Publishers Ltd; p. 88 (Fig 4.1), Corbis; p.89 (Fig 4.2), Wide World Photo, Inc; p.91 (Fig 4.3), The Bettman Archive; p.132 (Fig 5.2), from Hofstede G. (1980) *Culture Consequences*, copyright © 1980 Sage Publications Inc., reprinted by permission of Sage Publications.

Every effort has been made to obtain necessary permission with reference to copyright material. The publishers apologise if inadvertently any sources remain unacknowledged and will be glad to make the necessary arrangements at the earliest opportunity.

AN INTRODUCTION TO PSYCHOLOGY AND ITS APPROACHES

Introduction and overview

Definitions of psychology have changed frequently during its relatively short history as a separate field of study. This reflects different, and sometimes conflicting, theoretical views regarding the nature of human beings and the most appropriate methods for investigating them. Whilst there have been (and still are) many such theoretical approaches, three of the most important are the *behaviourist, psychodynamic* and *humanistic*. These, and the *neurobiological* (*biogenic*) and *cognitive* approaches, together form the core of what is commonly referred to as *mainstream* psychology.

Before looking at these approaches in detail, this chapter considers the discipline of psychology as a whole by looking at major areas of academic research and applied psychology.

What is psychology?

The word *psychology* is derived from the Greek *psyche* (mind, soul or spirit) and *logos* (discourse or study). Literally, then, psychology is the 'study of the mind'. The emergence of psychology as a separate discipline is generally dated at 1879, when Wilhelm Wundt opened the first psychological laboratory at the University of Leipzig in Germany. Wundt and his co-workers were attempting to investigate 'the mind' through *introspection* (observing and analysing the structure of their own conscious mental processes). Introspection's aim was to analyse conscious thought into its basic elements and perception into its constituent sensations, much as chemists analyse compounds into elements. This attempt to identify the structure of conscious thought is called *structuralism*.

Wundt and his co-workers recorded and measured the results of their introspections under controlled conditions, using the same physical surroundings, the same 'stimulus' (such as a clicking metronome), the same verbal instructions to each participant, and so on. This emphasis on measurement and control marked the separation of the 'new psychology' from its parent discipline of philosophy.

For hundreds of years, philosophers discussed 'the mind'. For the first time, scientists (Wundt was actually a physiologist by training) applied some of scientific investigation's basic methods to the study of mental processes. This was reflected in James's (1890) definition of psychology as:

> ' ... the Science of Mental Life, both of its phenomena and of their conditions ... The Phenomena are such things as we call feelings, desires, cognition, reasoning, decisions and the like'.

However, by the early twentieth century, the validity and usefulness of introspection were being seriously questioned, particularly by an American psychologist, John B. Watson. Watson believed that the results of introspection could never be proved or disproved, since if one person's introspection produced different results from another's, how could we ever decide which was correct? *Objectively*, of course, we cannot, since it is impossible to 'get behind' an introspective report to check its accuracy. Introspection is *subjective* and only the individual can observe his/her own mental processes.

Consequently, Watson (1913) proposed that psychologists should confine themselves to studying *behaviour*, since only this is measurable and observable by more than one person. Watson's form of psychology was known as *behaviourism*. It largely replaced introspectionism and advocated that people should be regarded as complex animals and studied using the same scientific methods as used by chemistry and physics. For Watson, the only way psychology could make any claims to being scientific was to emulate the natural sciences, and adopt its own objective methods. He defined psychology as:

' ... that division of Natural Science which takes human behaviour – the doings and sayings, both learned and unlearned – as its subject matter' (Watson, 1919).

The study of inaccessible, private, mental processes was to have no place in a truly scientific psychology.

Especially in America, behaviourism (in one form or another) remained the dominant force in psychology for the next 40 years or so. The emphasis on the role of learning (in the form of *conditioning*) was to make that topic one of the central areas of psychological research as a whole (see Box 1.8, pages 18–19).

Box 1.1 *Psychoanalytic theory and Gestalt psychology*

In 1900, Sigmund Freud, a neurologist living in Vienna, first published his *psychoanalytic theory* of personality in which the unconscious mind played a crucial role. In parallel with this theory, he developed a form of psychotherapy called *psychoanalysis*. Freud's theory (which forms the basis of the *psychodynamic* approach) represented a challenge and a major alternative, to behaviourism (see this chapter, pages 22–27).

A reaction against both structuralism and behaviourism came from the *Gestalt* school of psychology, which emerged in the 1920s in Austria and Germany. Gestalt psychologists were mainly interested in perception, and believed that perceptions could not be broken down in the way that Wundt proposed and behaviourists advocated for behaviour. Gestalt psychologists identified several 'laws' or principles of perceptual organisation (such as 'the whole is greater than the sum of its parts') which have made a lasting contribution to our understanding of the perceptual process (see Gross & McIlveen, 1998, for a detailed discussion).

In the late 1950s, many British and American psychologists began looking to the work of computer scientists to try to understand more complex behaviours which, they felt, had been either neglected altogether or greatly oversimplified by learning theory (conditioning). These complex behaviours were what Wundt, James and other early scientific psychologists had called '*mind*' or mental processes, but which were now referred to as *cognition* or *cognitive processes* (all the ways in which we come to know the world around us, how we attain, retain and regain information, through the processes of perception, attention, memory, problem-solving, language and thinking in general).

Cognitive psychologists see people as *information-processors,* and cognitive psychology has been heavily influenced by computer science, with human cognitive processes being compared with the operation of computer programs (the *computer analogy*). Cognitive psychology now forms part of *cognitive science,* which emerged in the late 1970s (see Figure 1.1, page 5). The events which together constitute the 'cognitive revolution' are described in Chapter 4 (page 95).

Although mental or cognitive processes can only be inferred from what a person does (they cannot be observed literally or directly), mental processes are now accepted as being valid subject-matter for psychology, provided they can be made 'public' (as in memory tests or problem-solving tasks). Consequently, what people say and do are perfectly acceptable sources of information about their cognitive processes, although the processes themselves remain inaccessible to the observer, who can study them only indirectly.

The influence of both behaviourism and cognitive psychology is reflected in Clark & Miller's (1970) definition of psychology as:

' ... the scientific study of behaviour. Its subject matter includes behavioural processes that are observable, such as gestures, speech and physiological changes, and processes that can only be inferred, such as thoughts and dreams'.

Similarly, Zimbardo (1992) states that:

'*Psychology* is formally defined as the scientific study of the behaviour of individuals and their mental processes ... '.

Classifying the work of psychologists

Despite behaviourist and cognitive psychology's influence on psychology's general direction in the last 80 years or so, much more

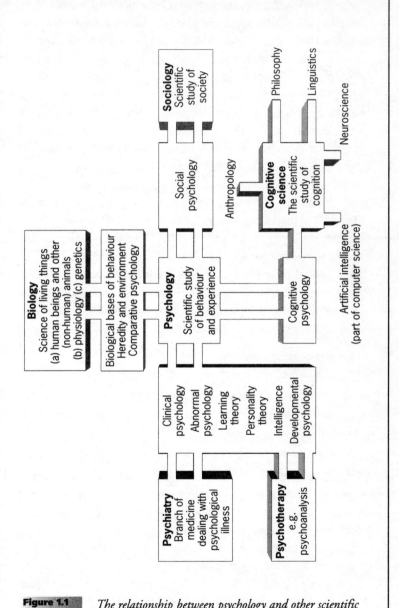

Figure 1.1 *The relationship between psychology and other scientific disciplines*

goes on within psychology than has been outlined so far. There are other theoretical approaches or orientations, other aspects of human (and non-human) activity that constitute the special focus of study, and different kinds of work that different psychologists do. A useful, but not hard and fast, distinction is that between the *academic* and *applied* branches of psychology (see Figure 1.3, page 17). Academic psychologists carry out research in a particular area and are attached to a university or research establishment where they will also teach undergraduates and supervise the research of postgraduates. Research is *pure* (done for its own sake and intended, primarily, to increase our knowledge and understanding) and *applied* (aimed at solving a particular problem). Applied research is usually funded by a government institution like the Home Office or the Department of Education and Employment, or by some commercial or industrial institution. The range of topics that may be investigated is as wide as psychology itself, but they may be classified as focusing either on the *processes* or *mechanisms* underlying various aspects of behaviour, or more directly on the *person* (Legge, 1975).

The process approach

This divides into four main areas: the biological bases of behaviour (or biopsychology), learning, cognitive processes and comparative psychology (the study of the behaviour of non-humans).

Biopsychology

Biopsychologists are interested in the physical basis of behaviour, how the functions of the nervous system (in particular the brain) and the endocrine (hormonal) system are related to and influence behaviour *and* mental processes. For example, are there parts of the brain specifically concerned with particular behaviours and abilities (*localisation of brain function*)? What role do hormones play in the experience of emotion and how are these linked to brain processes? What is the relationship between brain activity and different *states of consciousness* (including *sleep*)?

A fundamentally important biological process with important implications for psychology is genetic transmission. The *heredity* and *environment* (or *nature–nurture*) *issue* draws on what geneticists have discovered about the characteristics that can be passed from parents to offspring, how this takes place and how genetic factors interact with environmental ones. Other biopsychological topics include *motivation* and *stress*. Sensory processes are also biological processes, but are often discussed in connection with perception.

Cognitive psychology

As was seen on page 4, cognitive (or mental) processes include *attention*, *memory*, *perception*, *language*, *thinking*, *problem-solving*, *reasoning* and *concept-formation* ('higher-order' mental activities). Although these are often studied for their own sake, they may have important practical implications too, such as understanding the memory processes involved in eyewitness testimony. Much of social psychology (classified here as belonging to the person category) is cognitive in flavour, that is, concerned with the mental processes involved in interpersonal perception (e.g. stereotyping) and is known as *social cognition*. Also, Piaget's theory (again, belonging to the person category) is concerned with *cognitive development*.

The investigation of *learning* permeates most areas of psychology, which partly reflects the influence of behaviourism (see above). However, whilst *social learning theorists* accept many of the basic principles of conditioning theory, they believe that conditioning alone cannot account for most human social behaviour, and have focused on *observational learning* (*modelling*) as an important additional learning process, especially in children. Most human learning is closely related to cognitive processes, such as language and perception, and *cognitive learning* is also displayed by chimpanzees (*insight learning*) and rats ('*mental maps*') (see Gross & McIlveen, 1998).

The person approach
Developmental psychology

Developmental psychologists study the biological, cognitive, social and emotional changes that occur in people over time. One significant change within developmental psychology during the past 25 years or so is the recognition that development is not confined to childhood and adolescence, but is a lifelong process (the *lifespan approach*). It is now generally accepted that adulthood is a developmental stage, distinct from childhood, adolescence and old age.

Developmental psychology is not an isolated or independent field and advances in it depend on progress within psychology as a whole, such as behavioural genetics, (neuro)physiological psychology, learning, perception and motivation. Conversely, although Piaget's theory of cognitive development, for example, was meant to map the changes that take place up to about 15 years of age, he is considered to have made a major contribution to psychology as a whole.

Figure 1.2   *Jean Piaget (1896–1980)*

Social psychology

Some psychologists would claim that 'all psychology is social psychology', because all behaviour takes place within a social context and, even when we are alone, our behaviour continues to be influenced by others. However, other people usually have a more immediate and direct influence upon us when we are actually in their presence (as in *leadership*, *conformity* and *obedience*).

Social psychology is also concerned with *interpersonal perception* (forming impressions of others and judging the causes of their behaviour), interpersonal attraction and intimate relationships, prejudice and discrimination, and pro- and anti-social behaviour (especially aggression).

Abnormal psychology and atypical development

These areas study the underlying causes of deviant behaviour and psychological abnormality. Major *mental disorders* include schizophrenia, depression, anxiety disorders and eating disorders. Abnormal psychology is closely linked with *clinical psychology*, one of the major *applied* areas of psychology (see below). Psychologists who study abnormality and clinical psychologists are also concerned with the effectiveness of different forms of treatment and therapies. As will be seen later, each major theoretical approach has contributed to both the explanation and treatment of mental disorders.

Comparing the process and person approaches

In practice, it is very difficult to separate the two approaches, even if it can be done theoretically. However, there are important *relative* differences between them.

Box 1.2 *Some important differences between the process and person approaches*

- The *process approach* is typically confined to the laboratory (where experiments are the method of choice), makes far greater experimental use of non-humans and assumes that psychological processes (particularly learning) are essentially the

---

same in *all* species and that any differences between species are only *quantitative* (differences of degree).

- The *person approach* makes much greater use of field studies (such as observing behaviour in its natural environment) and of non-experimental methods (e.g. correlational studies). Typically, human participants are studied, and it is assumed that there are *qualitative* differences (differences in kind) between humans and non-humans.

Areas of applied psychology

Discussion of the person/process approaches has been largely concerned with the *academic* branch of psychology. Since the various areas of *applied* psychology are all concerned with people, they can be thought of as the applied aspects of the person approach. According to Hartley & Branthwaite (1997), most applied psychologists work in four main areas: *clinical*, *educational*, *occupational* and *government service* (such as prison psychologists). Additionally, Coolican (1996) identifies *criminological* (or *forensic*), *sports*, *health* and *environmental* psychologists. Hartley and Branthwaite argue that the work psychologists do in these different areas has much in common: it is the subject matters of their jobs which differ, rather than the skills they employ. Consequently, they consider an applied psychologist to be a person who can deploy specialised skills appropriately in different situations.

Box 1.3 *Seven major skills (or roles) used by applied psychologists*

- *The psychologist as counsellor:* helping people to talk openly, express their feelings, explore problems more deeply and see these problems from different perspectives. Problems may include school phobia, marriage crises and traumatic experiences (such as being the victim of a hijacking), and the counsellor can adopt a more or less *directive* approach (see page 30).
- *The psychologist as colleague:* working as a member of a team and bringing a particular perspective to a task, namely drawing attention to the human issues, such as the point of view of the

individual end-user (be it a product or a service of some kind).

- *The psychologist as expert:* drawing upon psychologists' specialised knowledge, ideas, theories and practical knowledge to advise on issues ranging from incentive schemes in industry to appearing as an 'expert witness' in a court case.
- *The psychologist as toolmaker:* using and developing appropriate measures and techniques to help in the analysis and assessment of problems. These include questionnaire and interview schedules, computer-based ability and aptitude tests and other *psychometric* tests (i.e. mental measurement).
- *The psychologist as detached investigator:* many applied psychologists carry out evaluation studies to assess the evidence for and against a particular point of view. This reflects the view of psychology as an objective science, which should use controlled experimentation whenever possible. The validity of this view is a recurrent theme throughout psychology (see, in particular, Chapter 4).
- *The psychologist as theoretician:* theories try to explain observed phenomena, suggesting possible underlying mechanisms or processes. They can suggest where to look for causes and how to design specific studies which will produce evidence for or against a particular point of view. Results from applied psychology can influence theoretical psychology and vice versa.
- *The psychologist as agent for change:* applied psychologists are involved in helping people, institutions and organisations, based on the belief that their work will change people and society for the better. However, some changes are much more controversial than others, such as the use of psychometric tests to determine educational and occupational opportunities (see Chapter 3) and the use of behaviour therapy and modification techniques to change abnormal behaviour (see Gross & McIlveen, 1998).

(Based on Hartley & Branthwaite, 1997)

Clinical psychology

Clinical psychologists are the largest single group of psychologists, both in the UK (Coolican, 1996) and America (Atkinson *et al.*, 1990). A related group is '*counselling psychologists*', who tend to work with younger clients in colleges and universities rather than in hospitals (see page 30).

Box 1.4 *The major functions of the clinical psychologist*

Clinical psychologists have had three years post-graduate training and their functions include:

- assessing people with learning difficulties, administering psychological tests to brain-damaged patients, devising rehabilitation programmes for long-term psychiatric patients, and assessing the elderly for their fitness to live independently.
- planning and carrying out programmes of therapy, usually *behaviour therapy/modification* (both derived from learning theory principles), or *psychotherapy* (group or individual) in preference to, or in addition to, behavioural techniques;
- carrying out research into abnormal psychology, including the effectiveness of different treatment methods ('outcome' studies). Patients are usually adults, many of whom will be elderly, in psychiatric hospitals, psychiatric wards in general hospitals and psychiatric clinics;
- involvement in community care as psychiatric care in general moves out of the large psychiatric hospitals;
- teaching other groups of professionals, such as nurses, psychiatrists and social workers.

Psychotherapy is usually carried out by *psychiatrists* (medically qualified doctors specialising in psychological medicine) or *psychotherapists* (who have undergone special training, including their own psychotherapy). In all its various forms, psychotherapy is derived from Freud's psychoanalysis (see below) and is distinguished both from behavioural treatments and physical treatments (those based on the medical model).

Criminological (or forensic) psychology

This is a branch of psychology which attempts to apply psychological principles to the criminal justice system. It is rooted in empirical research and draws on cognitive, developmental, social and clinical psychology. One main focus is the study of criminal behaviour and its management, but in recent years research interests have expanded to other areas, most notably those with a high media profile.

Box 1.5 *Some recent areas of research interest among criminological psychologists*

- Jury selection
- The presentation of evidence
- Eyewitness testimony
- Improving the recall of child witnesses
- False memory syndrome and recovered memory
- Offender profiling
- Crime prevention
- Devising treatment programmes (such as anger management)
- Assessing the risk of releasing prisoners

(From Coolican, 1996)

Criminological psychologists work in a wide range of contexts, including psychiatric hospitals and special hospitals for the criminally insane (such as Broadmoor and Rampton), young offender institutions and prisons. Like clinical psychologists, a crucial part of their work involves research and evaluation of what constitutes successful treatment.

Educational psychology

Educational psychologists have had at least two years teaching experience and gained a postgraduate qualification in educational or child psychology.

Box 1.6 *Some of the responsibilities of the educational psychologist*

- administering psychometric tests, particularly intelligence (or IQ) tests, as part of the assessment of learning difficulties;
- planning and supervising remedial teaching;
- research into teaching methods, the curriculum (subjects taught), interviewing and counselling methods and techniques;
- planning educational programmes for those with mental and physical impairments (including the visually impaired and autistic), and other groups of children and adolescents who are not attending ordinary schools (*special educational needs*);

- advising parents and teachers how to deal with children and adolescents with physical impairments, behaviour problems or learning difficulties;
- teacher training.

Educational psychologists are usually employed by a Local Education Authority (LEA) and work in one or more of the following: child and family centre teams (what was called 'child guidance'), the Schools Psychological Service, hospitals, day nurseries, nursery schools, special schools (day and residential) and residential children's homes. Clients are aged up to 18 years, but most fall into the 5 to 16 age-group.

Occupational (work or organisational) psychology

Occupational psychologists are involved in the selection and training of individuals for jobs and vocational guidance, including administration of aptitude tests and tests of interest. (This overlaps with the work of those trained in *personnel management*).

Box 1.7 *Other responsibilities of the occupational psychologist*

- helping people who, for reasons of illness, accident or redundancy, need to choose and re-train for a new career (industrial rehabilitation);
- designing training schemes, as part of *'fitting the person to the job'*. Teaching machines and simulators (such as of an aeroplane cockpit) often feature prominently in these;
- *'fitting the job to the person'* (*human engineering/ engineering psychology* or *ergonomics*), wherein applications from experimental psychology are made to the design of equipment and machinery in order to make the best use of human resources and to minimise accidents and fatigue. Examples include telephone dialling codes (memory and attention) and the design of decimal coinage (tactile and visual discrimination);
- advising on working conditions in order to maximise productivity (another facet of *ergonomics* – the study of people's efficiency in their working environments). Occupational groups

involved include computer/VDU operators, production line workers and air traffic controllers;

- helping the flow of communication between departments in government institutions, or 'industrial relations' in commerce and industry (*organisational psychology*). The emphasis is on the social, rather than the physical or practical, aspects of the working environment;
- helping to sell products and services through advertising and promotions. Many psychologists are employed in the advertising industry, where they draw on what experimental psychologists have discovered about human motivation, attitudes, cognition and so on (see Chapter 3).

Chartered psychologists

Since 1987, the British Psychological Society (BPS), the only professional body for British psychologists incorporated by Royal Charter, has been authorised under its Charter to keep a Register of Chartered Psychologists. Entry to the Register is restricted to members of the Society who have applied for registration, and who have the necessary qualifications or experience to have reached a standard sufficient for professional practice in psychology without supervision (Gale, 1990).

Major theoretical approaches in psychology

Different psychologists make different assumptions about what particular aspects of a person are worthy of study, and this helps to determine an underlying model or image of what people are like. In turn, this model or image determines a view of psychological normality, the nature of development, preferred methods of study, the major cause(s) of abnormality, and the preferred methods and goals of treatment.

An approach is a perspective which is not as clearly outlined as a theory and which:

' ... provides a general orientation to a view of humankind. It says, in effect, 'we see people as operating according to these basic principles and we therefore see explanations of human behaviour as

needing to be set within these limits and with these or those principles understood ... ' (Coolican, 1996).

As will be seen in the remainder of this chapter, all the major approaches include two or more distinguishable theories, but within an approach, they share certain basic principles and assumptions which give them a distinct 'flavour' or identity. The focus here is on the *behaviourist, psychodynamic* and *humanistic* approaches.

The behaviourist approach

Basic principles and assumptions

As seen on pages 2–3, Watson (1913) revolutionised psychology by rejecting the introspectionist approach and advocating the study of observable behaviour. Only by modelling itself on the natural sciences could psychology legitimately call itself a science. Watson was seeking to transform the very subject matter of psychology (from 'mind' to behaviour) and this is often called *methodological behaviourism*. According to Skinner (1987),

"Methodological' behaviourists often accept the existence of feelings and states of mind, but do not deal with them because they are not public and hence statements about them are not subject to confirmation by more than one person ... '.

In this sense, what was revolutionary when Watson (1913) first delivered his 'behaviourist manifesto' has become almost taken-for-granted, 'orthodox' psychology. It could be argued that *all* psychologists are methodological behaviourists (Blackman, 1980). Belief in the importance of empirical methods, especially the experiment, as a way of collecting data about humans (and non-humans), which can be quantified and statistically analysed, is a major feature of mainstream psychology (see Chapter 4). By contrast, as Skinner (1987) asserts:

' ... 'Radical' behaviourists ... recognise the role of private events (accessible in varying degrees to self-observation and physiological research), but contend that so-called mental activities are metaphors or explanatory fictions and that behaviour attributed to them can be more effectively explained in other ways ... '.

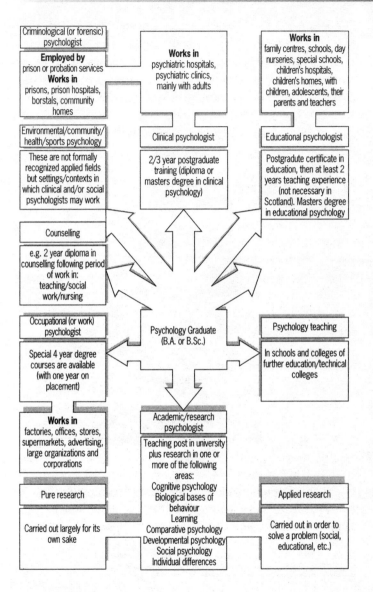

Figure 1.3 *The main areas of academic and applied psychology open to psychology graduates*

For Skinner, these more effective explanations of behaviour come in the form of the principles of reinforcement derived from his experimental work with rats and pigeons. What is 'radical' about Skinner's radical behaviourism is the claim that feelings, sensations and other private events cannot be used to explain behaviour but are to *be explained* in an analysis of behaviour. Whilst methodological behaviourism proposes to ignore such inner states (they are *inaccessible*), Skinner ignores them only as variables used for explaining behaviour (they are *irrelevant*), and argues that they can be translated into the language of reinforcement theory (Garrett, 1996).

Figure 1.4   *B.F. Skinner (1904–90)*

Given this important distinction between methodological and radical behaviourism, we need to consider some principles and assumptions that apply to behaviourism in general.

Box 1.8   *Basic principles and assumptions made by the behaviourist approach*

- Emphasis on the role of environmental factors in influencing behaviour, to the near exclusion of innate or inherited factors. This amounts essentially to a focus on learning. The key form of learning is conditioning, either classical (*Pavlovian* or *respondent*), which formed the basis of Watson's behaviourism, or operant (*instrumental*), which is at the centre of Skinner's radical behaviourism. Classical and operant conditioning are often referred to (collectively) as *learning theory*, as opposed to 'theories of learning' (which usually implies theories other than conditioning theories, that is, non-behaviourist theories).

- Behaviourism is often referred to as 'S–R' psychology ('S' standing for 'stimulus' and 'R' for 'response'). Whilst classical and operant conditioning account for observable behaviour (responses) in terms of environmental events (stimuli), the stimulus and response relationship is seen in fundamentally different ways. Only in classical conditioning is the stimulus seen as triggering a response in a predictable, automatic way, and it is this which is conveyed by 'S–R' psychology. It is, therefore, a mistake to describe operant conditioning as a 'S–R' approach.

- Both types of conditioning are forms of *associative learning*, whereby associations or connections are formed between stimuli and responses that did not exist before learning took place. This reflects the philosophical roots of behaviourism, namely the empirist philosophy of John Locke, which was a major influence on the development of science in general, as well as on behaviourism in particular (see Chapter 4).

- Part of Watson's rejection of introspectionism was his belief that it invoked too many vague concepts that are difficult, if not impossible, to define and measure. According to the *law of parsimony* (or 'Occam's razor'), the fewer assumptions a theory makes the better (more 'economical' explanations are superior).

- The mechanisms proposed by a theory should be as simple as possible. Behaviourists stress the use of *operational definitions* (defining concepts in terms of observable, measurable, events).

- The aim of a science of behaviour is to *predict* and *control* behaviour. This raises both *conceptual* questions (about the nature of science, in particular the role of theory: see Chapter 4) and *ethical* questions (for example, about power and the role of psychologists as agents of change: see Chapter 6).

Theoretical contributions

Behaviourism made a massive contribution to psychology, at least up to the 1950s, and explanations of behaviour in conditioning terms recur throughout the subject. For example, imagery as a form of organisation in memory and as a memory aid is based on the principle of association, and the interference theory of forgetting is largely couched in stimulus–response terms. Language, moral and gender development have all been explained in terms of conditioning, and some influential theories of the formation and maintenance of relationships focus on the concept of reinforcement. The behaviourist approach also offers one of the major models of abnormal behaviour. Finally, Skinner's notorious views on free will are discussed in detail in Chapter 2.

As with Freud's psychoanalytic theory (see below), theorists and researchers critical of the original, 'orthodox' theories have modified and built on them, making a huge contribution in the process. Noteworthy examples are Tolman's (1948) *cognitive behaviourism,* and *social learning theory.*

Practical contributions

We may think of *methodological behaviourism*, with its emphasis on experimentation, operational definitions, and the measurement of observable events (see Box 1.8), as a major influence on the practice of scientific psychology in general (what Skinner, 1974, called the 'science of behaviour'), quite unrelated to any views about the nature and role of mental events. Other, more 'tangible' contributions include:

- *behaviour therapy* and *behaviour modification* (based on *classical* and *operant conditioning* respectively) as major approaches to the treatment of abnormal behaviour and one of the main tools in the 'kit bag' of the clinical psychologist (see Box 1.4);
- *biofeedback* as a non-medical treatment for stress-related symptoms, derived from attempts to change rats' autonomic physiological functions through the use of operant techniques;
- *teaching machines* and *programmed learning*, which now commonly take the form of *computer assisted learning* (CAL).

An evaluation of behaviourism

In addition to the criticisms – both general and specific – which occur in the particular areas where behaviourist explanations are given, two evaluative points will be made here. The first concerns the famous 'Skinner box', the 'auto-environmental chamber' in which rats' and pigeons' environments can be totally controlled by the experimenter. Since pressing the lever was intended to be equivalent to a cat operating an escape latch in Thorndike's puzzle box, counting the number of lever presses (frequency of response) became the standard measure of operant learning. Despite Skinner's claims to not having a *theory*, 'the response' in operant conditioning has largely considered *only* the frequency of behaviour, ignoring intensity, duration and quality. As Glassman (1995) observes,

'While the focus on frequency was a practical consideration, it eventually became part of the overall conceptual framework as well – a case of research methods directing theory'.

But in everyday life, frequency is not always the most meaningful aspect of behaviour. For example, should we judge an artist's worth by *how many* paintings he or she produces, rather than their *content*?

The second criticism relates to Skinner's claim that human behaviour can be predicted and controlled in the same way as the behaviour of non-humans. Possessing language allows us to communicate with each other and to think about 'things' that have never been observed (and may not even exist), including rules, laws and principles (Garrett, 1996). Whilst these can only be expressed in words or thought about by means of words, much of people's behaviour is governed by them. According to Garrett, when this happens,

' ... behaviour is now shaped by what goes on inside their [people's] heads ... and not simply by what goes on in the external environment ... '.

What people *think* is among the important variables determining what they do and say, the very opposite of what Skinner's radical behaviourism claims.

The psychodynamic approach

The term 'psychodynamic' denotes the active forces within the personality that motivate behaviour and the inner causes of behaviour (in particular the unconscious conflict between the different structures that compose the whole personality). Whilst Freud's was the original psychodynamic theory, the approach includes all those theories based on his ideas, such as those of Jung (1964), Adler (1927) and Erikson (1950). Freud's *psychoanalytic theory* (sometimes called 'psychoanalysis') is psychodynamic, but the psychodynamic theories of Jung and so on, are not psychoanalytic. So the two terms are not synonymous. However, because of their enormous influence, Freud's ideas will be emphasised in the rest of this section.

Basic principles and assumptions

Freud's concepts are closely interwoven, making it difficult to know where their description should begin (Jacobs, 1992). Fortunately, Freud himself stressed acceptance of certain key theories as essential to the practice of psychoanalysis, the form of psychotherapy he pioneered and from which most others are derived (see below).

Box 1.9 *The major principles and assumptions of psychoanalytic theory*

- Much of our behaviour is determined by *unconscious* thoughts, wishes, memories and so on. What we are consciously aware of at any one time represents the tip of an iceberg: most of our thoughts and ideas are either not accessible at that moment (*preconscious*) or are totally inaccessible (*unconscious*). These unconscious causes can become conscious through the use of special techniques, such as *free association*, *dream interpretation* and *transference*, the cornerstones of *psychoanalysis* (see text below).
- Much of what is unconscious has been made so through *repression*, whereby threatening or unpleasant experiences are 'forgotten'. They become inaccessible, locked away from our conscious awareness. This is a major form of *ego defence*. Freud singled it out as a special cornerstone 'on which the whole

structure of psychoanalysis rests. It is the most essential part of it ... ' (Freud, 1914). Repression is closely related to *resistance*, interpretation of which is another key technique used in psychoanalysis.

- According to the *theory of infantile sexuality*, the sexual instinct or drive is active from birth and develops through a series of five *psychosexual stages*. The most important of these is the *phallic stage* (spanning the ages 3–5/6), during which all children experience the *Oedipus complex*. In fact, Freud used the German word *'Trieb'*, which translates as 'drive', rather than *'Instinkt'*, which was meant to imply that experience played a crucial role in determining the 'fate' of sexual (and aggressive) energy.
- Related to infantile sexuality is the general impact of early experience on later personality. According to Freud (1949),

  'It seems that the neuroses are only acquired during early childhood (up to the age of six), even though their symptoms may not make their appearance until much later ... the child is psychologically father of the man and ... the events of its first years are of paramount importance for its whole subsequent life.'

Figure 1.5   *Sigmund Freud (1856–1939)*

Theoretical contributions

As with behaviourist accounts of conditioning, many of Freud's ideas and concepts have become part of mainstream psychology's vocabulary. You do not have to be a 'Freudian' to use concepts such as repression, unconscious and so on, and many of the vast number of studies of different aspects of the theory have been conducted by critics hoping to discredit it (such as Eysenck, 1985; Eysenck & Wilson, 1973).

Like behaviourist theories, Freud's can also be found throughout psychology as a whole. His contribution is extremely rich and diverse, offering theories of motivation, dreams and the relationship between sleep and dreams, forgetting, attachment and the effects of early experience, moral and gender development, aggression and abnormality. Psychoanalytic theory has also influenced Gould's (1978, 1980) theory of the evolution of adult consciousness and Adorno *et al.*'s (1950) theory of the authoritarian personality (a major account of prejudice).

Finally, and as noted earlier, Freud's theories have stimulated the development of alternative theories, often resulting from the rejection of some of his fundamental principles and assumptions, but reflecting his influence enough for them to be described as psychodynamic.

Box 1.10   *Some major alternative psychodynamic theories to Freud's psychoanalytic theory*

- *Ego psychology*, promoted by Freud's daughter, Anna, focused on the mechanisms used by the ego to deal with the world, especially the *ego defence mechanisms*. Freud, by contrast, stressed the influence of the id's innate drives (especially sexuality and aggression) and is often described as an instinct theorist (but see Box 1.9, third point).
- Erik Erikson, trained by Anna Freud as a child psychoanalyst, also stressed the importance of the ego, as well as the influence of social and cultural factors on individual development. He pioneered the *lifespan approach* to development, proposing eight

psychosocial stages, in contrast with Freud's five *psychosexual* stages that end with physical maturity).

- Two of Freud's original 'disciples', Carl Jung and Alfred Adler, broke ranks with Freud and formed their own 'schools' ('*analytical psychology*' and '*individual psychology*' respectively). Jung attached relatively little importance to childhood experiences (and the associated personal unconscious) but considerable importance to the *collective* (or racial) unconscious, which stems from the evolutionary history of human beings as a whole.

- Like Jung, Adler rejected Freud's emphasis on sexuality, stressing instead the will to power or striving for superiority, which he saw as an attempt to overcome feelings of inferiority faced by all children as they grow up. He also shared Jung's view of the person as an indivisible unity or whole, and Erikson's emphasis on the social nature of human beings.

- Melanie Klein (1932) is often seen as a key transitional figure between Freud's instinct theory and the object relations school (see below). Like Anna Freud, she adapted Freud's techniques (such as pioneering *play therapy*) in order to tap a young child's unconscious, and maintained that the superego and Oedipus complex appear as early as the first and second years of life.

- The object relations school (the 'British school') was greatly influenced by Klein's emphasis on the infant's earliest relationships with its mother. It places far less emphasis on the role of instincts and more on the relationship with particular love objects (especially the mother), seeing early *relationships* as crucial for later development. Fairbairn (1952), for example, saw the aim of the libido as *object-seeking* (as opposed to pleasure-seeking), and this was extended by Bowlby (1969) in his *attachment theory*.

(Based on Jacobs, 1992; Holmes, 1993; Glassman, 1995; Fancher, 1996)

(a)　　　　(b)　　　　(c)　　　　(d)

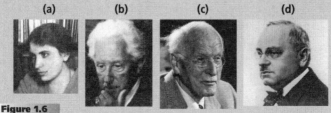

Figure 1.6

a Anna Freud (1895–1982); b Erik Erikson (1902–1994;
c Carl Gustav Jung (1875–1961); d Alfred Adler (1870–1937)

Practical contributions

The current psychotherapy scene is highly diverse, with only a minority using Freudian techniques, but, as Fancher (1996) points out:

> 'Most modern therapists use techniques that were developed either by Freud and his followers or by dissidents in explicit reaction against his theories. Freud remains a dominating figure, for or against whom virtually all therapists feel compelled to take a stand'.

Both Rogers, the major humanistic therapist (see below) and Wolpe (1958), who developed *systematic desensitisation* (a major form of behaviour therapy), were originally trained in Freudian techniques. Perls (1967), the founder of *Gestalt therapy*, Ellis (1958), the founder of *rational–emotive therapy* (RET), and Berne (1964), who devised *transactional analysis*, were also trained psychoanalysts.

Even Freud's fiercest critics concede his influence, not just within world psychiatry but in philosophy, literary criticism, history, theology, sociology and art and literature generally. Freudian terminology is commonly used in conversations between therapists well beyond Freudian circles, and his influence is brought daily to therapy sessions as part of the cultural background and experience of nearly every client (Jacobs, 1992).

An evaluation of the psychodynamic approach

A criticism repeatedly made of Freudian (and other psychodynamic) theories is that they are unscientific because they are *unfalsifiable* (incapable of being disproved). For example, if the Freudian prediction that 'dependent' men will prefer big-breasted women is confirmed, then the theory is supported. However, if such men actually prefer small-breasted women (Scodel, 1957), Freudians can use the concept of *reaction formation* (an ego defence mechanism) to argue that an unconscious fixation with big breasts may manifest itself as a conscious preference for the opposite, a clear case of ' heads I win, tails you lose' (Popper, 1959; Eysenck, 1985).

Figure 1.7   *Hans J. Eysenck (1916–1997), a major critic of Freud*

However, it is probably a mistake to see reaction formation as typical of Freudian theory as a whole. According to Kline (1989), for example, the theory comprises a collection of hypotheses, some of which are more easily tested than others, some of which are more central to the theory than others, and some of which have more supporting evidence than others.

Furthermore, Freud's theory provides methods and concepts which enable us to interpret and 'unpack' underlying meanings (it has great *hermeneutic strength*). Popper's and Eysenck's criticism helps to underline the fact that these meanings (both conscious and unconscious) cannot be measured in any precise way. Freud offers a way of understanding that is different from theories that are easily testable, and which may actually be *more* appropriate for capturing the nature of human experience and action (Stevens, 1995: see Chapter 4). According to Fancher (1996),

'Although always controversial, Freud struck a responsive chord with his basic image of human beings as creatures in conflict, beset by irreconcilable and often unconscious demands from within as well as without. His ideas about repression, the importance of early experience and sexuality, and the inaccessibility of much of human nature to ordinary conscious introspection have become part of the standard Western intellectual currency'.

The humanistic approach

Basic principles and assumptions

As has been seen, Rogers, a leading humanistic psychologist (and therapist) was trained as a psychoanalyst. Although the term 'humanistic psychology' was coined by Cohen (1958), a British psychologist, this approach emerged mainly in the USA during the 1950s. Maslow (1968), in particular, gave wide currency to the term 'humanistic' in America, calling it a 'third force' (the other two being behaviourism and Freudianism). However, Maslow did not reject these approaches but hoped to unify them, thus integrating both subjective and objective, the private and public aspects of the person, and providing a complete, holistic psychology.

Box 1.11 *Some basic principles and assumptions of the humanistic approach*

- Both the psychoanalytic and behaviourist approaches are *deterministic*. People are driven by forces beyond their control, either unconscious forces from within (Freud) or reinforcements from without (Skinner). Humanistic psychologists believe in *free will* and people's ability to choose how they act (see Chapter 2).

- A truly scientific psychology must treat its subject matter as fully human, which means acknowledging individuals as interpreters of themselves and their world. Behaviour, therefore, must be understood in terms of the individual's *subjective experience*, from the perspective of the actor (a *phenomenological* approach, which explains why this is sometimes called the 'humanistic-phenomenological' approach). This contrasts with the *positivist* approach (of the natural sciences), which tries to study people from the position of a detached observer. Only the individual can explain the meaning of a particular behaviour and is the 'expert' – not the investigator or therapist.

- Maslow argued that Freud supplied the 'sick half' of psychology, through his belief in the inevitability of conflict, neurosis, innate self-destructiveness and so on, whilst he (and Rogers) stressed the 'healthy half'. Maslow saw *'self-actualisation'* at the peak of a hierarchy of needs (see below), whilst Rogers talked about the

---

actualising tendency, an intrinsic property of life, reflecting the desire to grow, develop and enhance our capacities. A fully functioning person is the ideal of growth. Personality development naturally moves towards healthy growth, unless it is blocked by external factors, and should be considered the norm.

- Maslow's contacts with Wertheimer and other Gestalt psychologists (see Box 1.1, page 3) led him to stress the importance of understanding the *whole* person, rather than separate 'bits' of behaviour.

(From Glassman, 1995)

Theoretical contributions

Maslow's *hierarchy of needs* distinguishes between motives shared by both humans and non-humans and those that are uniquely human, and can be seen as an extension of the psychodynamic approach. Freud's id would represent physiological needs (at the hierarchy's base), Horney (a major critic of the male bias in Freud's theory: see Chapter 5) focused on the need for safety and love (corresponding to the next two levels), and Adler stressed esteem needs (at the next, fourth level). Maslow added self-actualisation to the peak of the hierarchy (Glassman, 1995).

Figure 1.8   *Abraham H. Maslow (1908–1970)*

According to Rogers (1951), whilst awareness of being alive is the most basic of human experiences, we each fundamentally live in a world of our own creation and have a unique perception of the world (the *phenomenal field*). It is our *perception* of external reality which shapes our lives (not external reality itself). Within our phenomenal field, the most significant element is our sense of *self*, 'an organised consistent gestalt, constantly in the process of forming and reforming' (Rogers, 1959). This view contrasts with many other self theorists who see it as a central, unchanging core of personality.

Practical contributions

By far the most significant practical influence of any humanistic psychologist is Rogers' *client-* (or *person-*) *centred therapy*. Less well known is the prolific research that Rogers undertook during the 1940s, 50s and 60s into this form of therapy. According to Thorne (1992),

'This body of research constituted the most intensive investigation of psychotherapy attempted anywhere in the world up to that time ... The major achievement of these studies was to establish beyond all question that psychotherapy could and should be subjected to the rigours of scientific enquiry'.

Figure 1.9 *Carl Rogers (1902–1987)*

Rogers helped develop research designs (such as Q-sorts), which enable objective measurement of the self-concept, ideal self, and their relationship over the course of therapy, as well as methodologies (such as rating scales and the use of external 'consultants') for exploring the importance of therapist *qualities*. These innovations continue to influence therapeutic practice, and many therapists are now concerned that their work should be subjected to research scrutiny. Research findings are now more likely than ever before to affect training procedures and clinical practice across many different therapeutic orientations (Thorne, 1992).

By emphasising the therapist's personal qualities, Rogers opened up psychotherapy to psychologists and contributed to the development of therapy provided by non-medically qualified thereapists (*lay therapy*). This is especially significant in the USA, where psychoanalysts *must* be psychiatrists (medically qualified). Rogers originally used the term 'counselling' as a strategy for silencing psychiatrists who objected to psychologists practising 'psychotherapy'. In the UK, the outcome of Rogers' campaign has been the evolution of a counselling profession whose practitioners are drawn from a wide variety of disciplines, with neither psychiatrists nor psychologists dominating. Counselling skills are used in a variety of settings throughout education, the health professions, social work, industry and commerce, the armed services and international organisations (Thorne, 1992).

Evaluation of the humanistic approach

According to Wilson *et al.* (1996), the humanistic approach is not an elaborate or comprehensive theory of personality, but should be seen as a set of uniquely personal theories of living created by humane people optimistic about human potential. It has wide appeal to those who seek an alternative to the more mechanistic, deterministic theories. However, like Freud's theory, many of its concepts are difficult to test empirically (such as self-actualisation), and it cannot account for the origins of personality. Since it describes but does not explain personality, it is subject to the *nominal fallacy* (Carlson & Buskist, 1997).

Nevertheless, for all its shortcomings, the humanistic approach represents a counterbalance to the psychodynamic (especially Freud) and the behaviourist approaches, and has helped to bring the 'person' back into psychology. Crucially, it recognises that people help determine their own behaviour and are not simply slaves to environmental contingencies or to their past. The self, personal responsibility and agency, choice and free will are now legitimate issues for psychological investigation.

Conclusions

Psychology is a diverse discipline. Psychologists investigate a huge range of behaviours and mental or cognitive processes. There is a growing number of applied areas, in which theory and research findings are brought to bear in trying to improve people's lives in a variety of ways. During the course of its life as a separate discipline, definitions of psychology have changed quite fundamentally, reflecting the influence of different theoretical approaches. This chapter has considered in detail the basic principles and assumptions of the behaviourist, psychodynamic and humanistic approaches, together with their theoretical and practical contributions to the discipline of psychology as a whole.

Summary

- Early psychologists, such as Wundt, attempted to study the mind through **introspection** under controlled conditions, aiming to analyse conscious thought into its basic elements (**structuralism**).
- Watson rejected introspectionism's subjectivity and replaced it with **behaviourism**. Only by regarding people as complex animals, using the methods of natural science and studying observable behaviour, could psychology become a true science.
- **Gestalt** psychologists criticised both structuralism and behaviourism, advocating that 'the whole is greater than the sum of

its parts'. Freud's **psychoanalytic theory** was another major alternative to behaviourism.

- Following the **cognitive revolution**, people came to be seen as **information-processors**, based on the **computer analogy**. Cognitive processes, such as perception and memory, became an acceptable part of psychology's subject-matter, even though they can only be inferred from behaviour.

- **Academic** psychologists are mainly concerned with conducting either **pure** or **applied research**, which may focus on underlying processes/mechanisms or on the person. The **process approach** consists of biopsychology, learning, cognitive processes and comparative psychology, whilst the **person approach** covers developmental, social and abnormal psychology.

- Although the process approach is largely confined to laboratory experiments using non-humans, the person approach makes greater use of field studies and non-experimental methods involving humans. The two approaches see species differences as **quantitative** or **qualitative** respectively.

- Most **applied** psychologists work in clinical, educational, occupational or government service, with newer fields including criminological/forensic, sports, health and environmental psychology. Common skills or roles shared by all these practitioners include counsellor, expert, toolmaker, detached investigator, theoretician and agent for change.

- **Clinical** psychologists are the most numerous group of applied psychologists. Their functions include planning and carrying out behaviour therapy/modification, as well as psychotherapy, which is more commonly carried out by psychiatrists and psychotherapists.

- The British Psychological Society keeps a Register of **Chartered Psychologists**, restricted to those with the necessary qualifications or experience for unsupervised professional practice.

- Different theoretical **approaches/perspectives** are based on different models/images of the nature of human beings.
- Watson's **methodological behaviourism** removes mental processes from the science of psychology and focuses on what can be quantified and observed by different researchers. Skinner's **radical behaviourism** regards mental processes as both **inaccessible** and **irrelevant** for explaining behaviour, but can **be explained** by the principles of reinforcement.
- The behaviourist approach stresses the role of environmental influences (learning), especially classical and operant **conditioning**. Behaviourists also advocate the **law of parsimony** and the use of **operational definitions**. Psychology's aim is to **predict** and **control** behaviour.
- Tolman's **cognitive behaviourism** and **social learning theory** represent modifications of 'orthodox' learning (conditioning) theory and have made huge contributions in their own right.
- Methodological behaviourism has influenced the practice of scientific psychology in general. Other practical contributions include behaviour therapy and modification, biofeedback and teaching machines/programmed learning.
- Whilst not formally part of a 'theory' of conditioning, counting the **frequency of response** in the Skinner box has become part of the overall conceptual framework of operant learning. This ignores intensity, duration and quality of response. Also, Skinner's claim that human behaviour can be predicted and controlled in the same way as that of non-humans is contradicted by the fact that thinking through language actually determines people's behaviour.
- The **psychodynamic approach** is based on Freud's **psychoanalytic theory**. Central aspects of Freud's theory are the **unconscious** (especially **repression**), **infantile sexuality** and the **impact of early experience** on later personality. The cornerstones of psychoanalysis are **free association**, **dream interpretation** and **transference**.

- Freud identified five stages of **psychosexual development**, the most important being the **phallic stage**, during which all children experience the **Oedipus complex**. This is relevant to explaining moral and gender development. Freud's ideas have become part of mainstream psychology, contributing to our understanding of motivation, sleep and dreams, forgetting, attachment, aggression and abnormality.

- Major modifications/alternatives to Freudian theory include **ego psychology**, Erikson's **psychosocial** developmental theory, Jung's 'analytical psychology', Adler's 'individual psychology' and the **object relations school**, influenced by Klein's focus on the infant's earliest relationship with the mother.

- All forms of psychotherapy stem directly or indirectly from psychoanalysis, and many trained psychoanalysts have been responsible for developing radically different therapeutic approaches, including Rogers, Perls and Wolpe.

- Freud's influence on a wide range of disciplines outside psychology and psychotherapy is undeniable, as is his more general impact on Western culture. Whilst his theory is often dismissed as **unfalsifiable** (and, therefore, unscientific), the criticism fails to acknowledge its great **hermeneutic strength**.

- Maslow called the **humanistic approach** the 'third force' in psychology. It believes in **free will**, the importance of taking the actor's perspective (the **phenomenological approach**), understanding the **whole person**, the positive aspects of human personality, and the natural tendency towards healthy growth.

- **Self-actualisation** is at the top of Maslow's hierarchy of needs, whilst for Rogers, the **self** is the most significant part of our **phenomenal field**, the only true reality for the individual.

- Rogers developed **client/person-centred therapy**. He was also a prolific researcher into the effectiveness of his therapy, inspiring others to do the same and influencing both therapist training and clinical practice. He opened up psychotherapy to psychologists and other non-medically qualified practitioners, and created a counselling profession that operates within a wide diversity of settings.

- The humanistic approach may be very difficult to test empirically, but it represents a major alternative to deterministic theories and has helped to bring the 'person' back into psychology.

THE NATURE OF THE PERSON IN PSYCHOLOGY: FREE WILL AND DETERMINISM, AND REDUCTIONISM

2

Introduction and overview

As Chapter 4 shows, any discussion of psychology's scientific status raises fundamental questions about the nature of the person or, at least, the image of the person that underlies major psychological theories (see Chapter 1) and which is implicit in much of the study of human behaviour. This chapter discusses two of these fundamental questions. One, debated by Western philosophers for centuries, is whether we choose to act as we do, or whether behaviours are caused by influences beyond our control (*free will versus determinism*). The other, which has a shorter history and is debated by philosophers of science, concerns the validity of attempts to explain complex wholes in terms of their constituent parts (*reductionism*). One example of this is the relationship between the mind or consciousness and the brain (the '*mind–body problem*').

Free will and determinism

What is free will?

One way of approaching this question is to consider examples of behaviour where 'free will' (however defined) is clearly *absent*.

Box 2.1   *A case of Tourette's disorder*

Tim is 14 and displays a variety of twitches and tics. His head sometimes jerks and he often blinks and grimaces. Occasionally, he blurts out words, usually vulgarities. He does not mean to do it and is

---

embarrassed by it, but he cannot control it. Because of his strange behaviour, most other children avoid him. His isolation and embarrassment are interfering with his social development. Tim suffers from a rare condition called Tourette's disorder.
(From Holmes, 1994)

EXERCISE 1

What specific aspects of Tim's disorder are relevant to understanding the concept of 'free will'? If you think Tim lacks it, what led you to this conclusion? Think of other behaviours (normal or abnormal) that demonstrate a lack of free will.

Intuition tells us that people have the ability to choose their own courses of action, determine their behaviours and, to this extent, have *free will*. Simultaneously, though, this freedom is exercised only within certain physical, political, sociological and other environmental constraints. However, the positivistic, mechanistic nature of scientific psychology (see Chapter 4) implies that behaviour is *determined* by external (or internal) events or stimuli and that people are passive responders. To this extent, people are *not* free. *Determinism* also implies that behaviour occurs in a regular, orderly manner which (in principle) is totally predictable. For Taylor (1963), determinism maintains that:

'in the case of everything that exists, there are antecedent conditions, known or unknown, given which that thing could not be other than it is ... More loosely, it says that everything, including every cause, is the effect of some cause or causes; or that everything is not only determinate but causally determined'.

'Everything that exists' includes people and their thoughts and behaviours, so a 'strict determinist' believes that thought and behaviours are no different from (other) 'things' or events in the world. However, this begs the question of whether thoughts and behaviours are the same *kind of thing or event* as, say, chemical reactions in a test tube, or neurons firing in the brain. We don't usually ask if the chemicals 'agreed' to combine in a certain way, or if the neurons 'decided' to fire. Unless we were trying to be witty, we would be guilty of *anthropomorphism* (attributing human abilities and characteristics to non-humans).

It is only *people* who can agree and make decisions. These abilities and capacities are part of our concept of a person, which, in turn, forms an essential part of 'everyday' or commonsense psychology (see Chapter 1). Agreeing and deciding are precisely the kinds of things we do *with our minds* (they are mental processes or events), and to be able to agree and make decisions, it is necessary to 'have a mind'. So, free will implies having a mind. However, having a mind does not imply free will: it is possible that decisions and so on are themselves *caused* (determined), even though they seem to be freely chosen.

EXERCISE 2

Try to explain what someone means when he or she says: 'I had no choice but to ...' or 'You leave me no choice ...'. Can you interpret this in a way that is consistent with a belief in free will?

Different meanings of 'free will'

One of the difficulties with the free will versus determinism debate is the ambiguity of the concepts involved.

Having a choice

The 'actor' could have behaved differently, given the same circumstances. This contrasts sharply with a common definition of determinism, namely that things could only have happenend as they did, given everything that happened previously.

Not being coerced or constrained

If someone puts a loaded gun to your head and tells you to do something, your behaviour is clearly not free: you have been *forced* to act this way. This is usually where the philosophical debate about 'free' will *begins*. It is also related to what James (1890) called *soft determinism* (see pages 45–46).

Voluntary

If 'involuntary' conveys reflex behaviour (such as the eye-blink response to a puff of air directed at the eye), then 'voluntary' implies 'free' (the behaviour is not automatic). By definition, most behaviour (human and non-human) is *not* reflex, nor is it usually the result of coercion. So is most behaviour free?

Box 2.2 *Evidence for the distinction between voluntary and involuntary behaviour*

Penfield's (1947) classic experiments involved stimulating the cortex of patients about to undergo brain surgery. Even though the cortical area being stimulated was the same as that which is involved when we normally ('voluntarily') move our limbs, patients reported feeling that their arms and legs were being moved passively, quite a different experience from initiating the movement themselves. This demonstrates that the *subjective experience* (phenomenology) of the voluntary movement of one's limbs cannot be *reduced* to the stimulation of the appropriate brain region (otherwise Penfield's patients should not have reported a difference). Doing things voluntarily simply *feels* different from the 'same' things 'just happening'. Similarly, Delgado (1969) stimulated a part of the primary motor area in a patient's left hemisphere, causing him to form a clenched fist with his right hand. When asked to try to keep his fingers still during the next stimulation of his cortex, the patient, unable to do this, commented, 'Doctor, your electricity is stronger than my will'.

If this is true for bodily movements, then it adds weight to the claim that having free will is an undeniable part of our subjective experience of ourselves as people. The sense of self is most acute (and important and real for us) where moral decisions and feelings of responsibility for past actions are involved (Koestler, 1967). See text and Box 2.3 for further discussion of free will and moral responsibility.

One demonstration of people's belief in their free will is *psychological reactance* (Brehm, 1966; Brehm & Brehm, 1981). A common response to the feeling that our freedom is being threatened is the attempt to regain or reassert it, which is related to the need to be free from others' controls and restrictions, to determine our own actions, and not be dictated to. A good deal of contrary (resistant) behaviour, otherwise known as 'bloody-mindedness' ('Don't tell me what to do!') seems to reflect this process (Carver & Scheier, 1992).

Similar to this need to feel free from others' control is *intrinsic motivation* or *self-determination* (Deci, 1980; Deci & Ryan, 1987). This refers to people's intrinsic interest in things, such that they do not need to be offered extrinsic incentives for doing them. Engaging in such activities is motivated by the desire for competence and self-determination.

So what happens if someone is offered an extrinsic reward for doing something which is already interesting and enjoyable in itself? Lepper *et al.* (1973) found that the activity loses its intrinsic appeal, and motivation is reduced (the *paradox of reward*). This has implications for accounts of moral development based on learning theory principles, especially operant conditioning.

EXERCISE 3

How could you account for the 'paradox of reward' in terms of attributional principles, specifically, internal and external causes?

Deliberate control

Norman & Shallice (1986) define divided attention as an upper limit to the amount of processing that can be performed on incoming information at any one time. They propose three levels of functioning, namely *fully automatic processing*, *partially automatic processing*, and *deliberate control*. Deliberate control corresponds to free will.

Driving a car is a sensory–motor skill, performed by experienced drivers more-or-less automatically. It does not require deliberate, conscious control, unless some unexpected event disrupts the performance (such as putting your foot on the brake when there is an obstacle ahead: this is a 'rule of the game').

However, on an icy road, this can be risky, since the steering wheel has a different 'feel' and the whole driving strategy must be changed. After doing it several times, this too may become a semi-automatic routine:

> 'but let a little dog amble across the icy road in front of the driver, and he will have to make a 'top-level decision' whether to slam down the brake, risking the safety of his passengers, or run over the dog. And if, instead of a dog, the jaywalker is a child, he will probably resort to the brake, whatever the outcome. It is at this level, when the pros and cons are equally balanced, that the subjective experience of freedom and moral responsibility arises' (Koestler, 1967).

As we move downwards from conscious control, the subjective experience of freedom diminishes. According to Koestler:

> 'Habit is the enemy of freedom ... Machines cannot become like men, but men can become like machines'.

Koestler also maintains that the second enemy of freedom is very powerful (especially negative) emotion:

> 'When [emotions] are aroused, the control of decisions is taken over by those primitive levels of the hierarchy which the Victorians called 'the Beast in us' and which are in fact correlated to phylogenetically older structures in the nervous system'.

The arousal of these structures results in 'diminished responsibility' and 'I couldn't help it' (Koestler, 1967).

EXERCISE 4

In Koestler's quote above, (a) what does 'phylogenetically older structures' mean? and (b) what are the major 'primitive levels of the hierarchy' correlated with these structures?

Why should psychologists be interested in the concept of free will?

As noted in the *Introduction and overview*, the philosophical debate about free will and determinism is centuries old. It can be traced back at least to the French philosopher Descartes (1596–1650), whose ideas had a great influence on both science in general and psychology in particular. For much of its history as a separate, scientific discipline, psychology has operated as if there were no difference between natural, physical phenomena and human thought and behaviour (see pages 52–53).

During the period 1913–1956, psychology (at least in the USA) was dominated by behaviourism, Skinner being particularly influential. Skinner's beliefs about the influence of mental phenomena on behaviour, and those concerning free will, are discussed on pages 48–51.

EXERCISE 5

Try to identify some (other) ways in which the issue of free will is relevant to psychological theory and practice. For example, how does the notion of free will relate to criteria for defining and diagnosing mental disorders?

Free will and psychological abnormality

Definitions of abnormality, and the diagnosis and treatment of mental disorders, often involve implicit or explicit judgements about free will and determinism. In a general sense, mental disorders can be seen as the partial or complete breakdown of the control people normally have over their thoughts, emotions and behaviours. For example, *compulsive* behaviour, by definition, is behaviour which a person cannot help but do: he or she is 'compelled' to do it. People are *attacked* by panic, *obsessed* by thoughts of germs, or become the *victims* of thoughts which are *inserted* into their mind from outside and are under external influence. In all these examples, things are happening to, or being done to, the individual (instead of the individual *doing them*), both from the individual's perspective and that of a psychologist or psychiatrist.

Being judged to have lost control (possession of which is usually thought of as a major feature of normality), either temporarily or permanently, is a legally acceptable defence in cases of criminal offences.

Box 2.3 *Forensic psychiatry, diminished responsibility and the law*

Forensic psychiatry deals with assessment and treatment of mentally disturbed offenders. The 1983 Mental Health Act has several clauses providing for the compulsory detention of prisoners (either while awaiting trial or as part of their sentences) in hospital. Psychiatrists, as expert witnesses, can play important roles in advising the Court about:

1 fitness to plead;
2 mental state at the time of the offence;
3 diminished responsibility.

The defence of *diminished responsibility* (for murder) was introduced in England and Wales in the 1957 Homicide Act, largely replacing the plea of 'not guilty by reason of insanity', which was based on the 'McNaughton Rules' of 1843.

If accepted, there is no trial and a sentence of manslaughter is passed. If not accepted, a trial is held and the jury must decide whether the accused (at the time the crime was committed) was suffering from an abnormality of mind, and if so, whether it was such as to substantially impair his or her responsibility.

Peter Sutcliffe, the 'Yorkshire Ripper', was found guilty of the murder of 13 women and the attempted murder of seven others, despite his defence that he heard God's voice telling him to 'get rid' of prostitutes. In finding him guilty of murder, the jury did not necessarily reject the defence's argument that he was suffering from paranoid schizophrenia, only that it did not constitute an abnormality of mind of sufficient degree to substantially impair his mental responsibility for his acts. Sutcliffe was sentenced to 20 concurrent terms of life imprisonment, which he served initially in an ordinary prison before being sent to Broadmoor Special Hospital.

(Based on Gelder *et al.*, 1989, and Prins, 1995)

Free will and moral accountability

Underlying the whole question of legal (and moral) responsibility is the presupposition that people are, at least some of the time, able to control their behaviours and choose between different courses of action. How else could we ever be held responsible for *any* of our actions? In most everyday situations and interactions, we attribute responsibility, both to ourselves and others, unless we have reason to doubt it. According to Flanagan (1984):

> 'it seems silly to have any expectations about how people ought to act, if everything we do is the result of some inexorable causal chain which began millenia ago. 'Ought', after all, seems to imply 'can', therefore, by employing a moral vocabulary filled with words like 'ought' and 'should', we assume that humans are capable of rising above the causal pressures presented by the material world, and, in assuming this we appear to be operating with some conception of freedom, some notion of free will'.

Free will as an issue in major psychological theories

Most major theorists in psychology have addressed the issue of free will and determinism, including James, Freud, Skinner, and Rogers.

James and soft determinism

As was seen in Chapter 1, James pioneered psychology as a separate, scientific discipline. In *The Principles of Psychology* (1890), he devoted a whole chapter to the 'will', which he related to attention:

> 'The most essential achievement of the will ... when it is most 'voluntary' is to *attend* to a different object and hold it fast before the mind ... Effort of attention is thus the essential phenomenon of will'.

For James, there was a conflict. Belief in determinism seemed to fit best with the scientific view of the world, whilst belief in free will seemed to be required by our social, moral, political, and legal practices, as well as by our personal, subjective experience (see above). His solution to this conflict was two-fold.

First, he distinguished between the scientific and non-scientific worlds. Psychology as a science could only progress by assuming determinism, but this does not mean that belief in free will must be abandoned in other contexts. So, scientific explanation is not the only useful kind of explanation.

Second, he drew a further distinction between *soft* and *hard* determinism. According to *soft determinism*, the question of free will depends on the type(s) of cause(s) our behaviour has, not whether it is caused or not caused (the opposite of 'not caused' is 'random', not 'free'). If our actions have, as their immediate (proximate) cause, processing by a system such as *conscious mental life* (or CML, which includes consciousness, purposefulness, personality and personal continuity), then they count as free, rational, voluntary, purposive actions.

According to *hard determinism*, CML is itself caused, so that the immediate causes are only part of the total causal chain which results in the behaviour we are trying to explain. Therefore, as long as our behaviour is caused at all, there is no sense in which we can be described as acting freely.

Freud and psychic determinism

Although in most respects their ideas about human behaviour are diametrically opposed, Freud and Skinner shared the fundamental belief that free will is an illusion. However, in keeping with their theories as a whole, their reasons are radically different.

EXERCISE 6

Based on what you already know about Freud's psychoanalytic theory, try to identify those parts which are most relevant to his rejection of free will.

According to Strachey (1962):

'Behind all of Freud's work ... we should posit his belief in the universal validity of the law of determinism ... Freud extended the belief (derived from physical phenomena) uncompromisingly to the field of mental phenomena'.

Similarly, Sulloway (1979) maintains that all of Freud's work in science (and Freud saw himself very much as a scientist) was characterised by an abiding faith in the notion that all vital phenomena, including psychical (psychological) ones, are rigidly and lawfully determined by the principle of cause and effect.

One major example of this was the extreme importance he attached to the technique of *free association*.

Box 2.4 *How 'free' is Freud's 'free association'?*

'Free association' is a misleading translation of the German *'freier Einfall'*, which conveys much more accurately the intended impression of an uncontrollable 'intrusion' ('Einfall') by pre-conscious ideas into conscious thinking. In turn, this pre-conscious material reflects *unconscious* ideas, wishes and memories (what Freud was really interested in), since here lie the principal cause(s) of neurotic problems.

It is a great irony that 'free' association should refer to a technique used in psychoanalysis meant to reveal the *unconscious causes* of behaviour. It is because the causes of our thoughts, actions and supposed choices are unconscious (mostly *actively repressed*), that we *think* we are free. Freud's application of this general philosophical belief in causation to mental phenomena is called *psychic determinism*.

(Based on Sulloway, 1979)

For Freud, part of what 'psychic determinism' conveyed was that in the universe of the mind, there are no 'accidents'. No matter how apparently random or irrational behaviour may be (such as 'parapraxes' or 'Freudian slips'), unconscious causes can always account for them, and this also applies to hysterical symptoms and dreams. As Gay (1988) states, '… Freud's theory of the mind is … strictly and frankly deterministic'. However:

- Freud accepted that true accidents, in the sense of forces beyond the victim's control (e.g. being struck by lightning), can and do occur, and are not unconsciously caused by the victim.
- One of the aims of psychoanalysis is to 'give the patient's ego *freedom* to decide one way or another' (Freud, quoted in Gay, 1988), so therapy rests on the belief that people *can* change. However, Freud saw the extent of possible change as being very limited.
- One aspect of psychic determinism is *overdetermination*, that is, much of our behaviour has *multiple* causes, both conscious

and unconscious. So, although our conscious choices, decisions and intentions may genuinely influence behaviour, they never tell the whole story.

- Despite never having predicted in advance what choice or decision a patient would make, Freud maintained that these are not arbitrary and can be understood as revealing personality characteristics (Rycroft, 1966). What Freud often did was to explain his patients' choices, neurotic symptoms, and so on *not* in terms of causes (the *scientific* argument), but by trying to make sense of them and give them meaning (the *semantic* argument). Indeed, the latter is supported by the title of, arguably, his greatest book, *The Interpretation of Dreams* (1900) (as opposed to *The 'Cause' of Dreams*).

Skinner and the illusion of free will

Like Freud, Skinner sees free will as an illusion. However, whilst Freud focused on 'the mind', especially unconscious thoughts, wishes, and memories, Skinner's *radical behaviourism* eliminates all reference to mental or private states as part of the explanation of behaviour (including theories like Freud's!).

Although Skinner does not deny that pain and other internal states exist, they have no 'causal teeth' and hence no part to play in scientific explanations of (human) behaviour (Garrett, 1996). Free will (and other '*explanatory fictions*') cannot be defined or measured objectively, nor are they needed for successful prediction and control of behaviour (for Skinner, the primary aims of a science of behaviour). It is only because the causes of human behaviour are often hidden from us in the environment, that the myth or illusion of free will survives.

EXERCISE 7

Given what you know about Skinner's theory of operant conditioning and his 'analysis of behaviour', try to identify the causes of human behaviour which he believes are often hidden from us in the environment (see Chapter 1).

Skinner argues that when what we do is dictated by force or punishment, or by their threat (negative reinforcement), it is obvious to everyone that we are not acting freely. For example, when the possibility of prison stops us committing crimes, there is clearly no choice involved, because we know what the environmental causes of our behaviour are. Similarly, it may sometimes be very obvious which positive reinforcers are shaping behaviour (a bonus for working over-time, for example).

However, most of the time we are unaware of environmental causes, and it looks (and feels) as if we are behaving freely. Yet all this means is that we are free of punishments or negative reinforcement, and behaviour is still determined by the pursuit of things that have been positively reinforced in the past. When we perceive others as behaving freely, we are simply unaware of their reinforcement histories (Fancher, 1996).

Box 2.5 *The freedom myth and the rejection of punishment*

In *Beyond Freedom and Dignity*, Skinner (1971) argued that the notion of 'autonomous man', upon which so many of Western society's assumptions are based, is both false and has many harmful consequences. In particular, the assumption that people are free *requires* that they are constantly exposed to punishment and its threat as a negative reinforcer (Fancher, 1996).

Based on experiments with rats and pigeons, Skinner argued that positive reinforcement is more effective than negative reinforcement or punishment in producing lasting conditioning effects. In Skinner's version of Utopia (described in his novel *Walden Two*, 1948), negative reinforcement is completely abandoned as a means of social control. Children are reared only to seek positive reinforcement contingent upon their showing socialised, civilised behaviour. Inevitably, they grow up to be cooperative, intelligent, sociable and happy.

EXERCISE 8

What *ethical* issues are raised by Skinner's advocacy of a utopian society like *Walden Two*? In what ways does this Utopia reflect Skinner's beliefs about the aims of a scientific psychology?

Skinner and moral responsibility

Clearly, Skinner's belief that free will is an illusion conflicts with the need to attribute people with free will if we are to hold them (and ourselves) morally (and legally) responsible for their behaviour. Skinner (1971) himself acknowledges that freedom and dignity are:

> 'essential to practices in which a person is held responsible for his conduct and given credit for his achievements'.

However, Skinner equates 'good' and 'bad' with 'beneficial to others' (what is rewarded) and 'harmful to others' (what is punished) respectively, thus removing morality from human behaviour. For Skinner, 'oughts' are not 'moral imperatives': they reflect *practical*, rather than moral, guidelines and rules (Morea, 1990).

According to Garrett (1996), if we are rational, thinking creatures capable of assessing ethical rules and principles and evaluating the goodness of our lives, then we have all the freedom needed to reasonably prefer democratic to non- (or anti-) democratic forms of government (as expressed in *Walden Two* and *Beyond Freedom and Dignity*).

A further consequence of Skinner's rejection of the notion of 'autonomous man' is what Ringen (1996) calls *the behaviour therapist's dilemma*, which is closely related to some of the most fundamental *ethical* issues faced by psychologists as *agents of change* (see Chapter 6, pages 164–170).

Box 2.6   *The behaviour therapist's dilemma*

Ringen (1996) claims that there is a deep tension between two features of modern clinical psychology. On the one hand, Skinner (1971) argues that scientific considerations support radical behaviourism as the most appropriate framework for understanding and facilitating the development of effective behaviour therapy (including methods based on both classical and operant conditioning). On the other hand, an increasingly significant ethical and legal constraint on therapeutic practice, the doctrine of informed consent, obliges behaviour therapists (and other practitioners in the helping professions, including psychiatry) to acknowledge the autonomy of those who come to them for help.

The *behaviour therapist's dilemma* describes a widely accepted assessment of why these two aspects of modern clinical psychology are in tension, namely, that *either* radical behaviourism is false or human beings never act autonomously. This involves having to choose between alternatives that many contemporary behaviour therapists would find it difficult to defend.

(From Ringen, 1996)

Rogers, freedom and the fully functioning person

As was seen in Chapter 1, Rogers was perhaps the most influential *humanistic, phenomenological* psychologist. As such, he stressed the process of self-actualisation and the necessity of adopting the other person's perspective if we are to understand that person, and in particular, his or her self-concept.

Understanding the self-concept is also central to Rogers' *client-centred therapy*. His experience as a therapist convinced him that real change does occur in therapy: people choose to see themselves and their life situations differently. Therapy and life are about free human beings struggling to become more free. Personal experience is important, but it does not imprison us. How we react to our experience is something we ourselves choose and decide (Morea, 1990).

EXERCISE 9

According to Rogers, in what ways are individuals prevented from recognising their *true* feelings and behaviour? In what respects is Rogers' view of human beings a more optimistic one than, say, Freud's?

Rogers' deep and lasting trust in human nature did not, however, blind him to the reality of evil *behaviour*:

'In my experience, every person has the capacity for evil behaviour. I, and others, have had murderous and cruel impulses ... feelings of

anger and rage, desires to impose our wills on others ... Whether I ... will translate these impulses into behaviour depends ... on two elements: social conditioning and voluntary choice' (Rogers, 1982, cited in Thorne, 1992).

By making the distinction between 'human nature' and behaviour, Rogers retains his optimistic view of human beings. However, this did not exclude altogether a deterministic element in his later writings. In *Freedom to Learn for the '80s* (1983), he states that it is becoming clear from science that human beings are complex machines and not free. So how can this be reconciled with self-actualisation, psychological growth, and the freedom to choose?

One proposed solution is in the form of a version of soft determinism. Unlike neurotic and incongruent people, whose defensiveness forces them to act in ways they would prefer not to, the healthy, fully functioning person:

'not only experiences, but utilises, the most absolute freedom when he spontaneously, freely and voluntarily chooses and wills that which is absolutely determined'.

The fully functioning person chooses to act and be the way he or she has to. It is the most satisfying way to behave (Morea, 1990).

Reductionism

What is reductionism?

Together with positivism, mechanism, determinism, and empiricism, reductionism represents part of 'classical' science (see Chapter 4). Luria (1987) traces the origins of reductionism to the mid-nineteenth century view within biology that the organism is a complex of organs and the organs are complexes of cells. To explain the basic laws of the living organism, we have to study as carefully as possible the features of separate cells.

From its biological origins, reductionism was extended to science in general. For example, the properties of a protein molecule could be uniquely determined or predicted in terms of properties of the electrons or protons making up its atoms. Consistent with this view is Garnham's (1991) definition of reductionism as:

'the idea that psychological explanations can be replaced by explanations in terms of brain functioning or even in terms of physics and chemistry'.

Although reductionism's ultimate aim (according to its supporters) is to account for all phenomena in terms of microphysics, *any* attempt to explain something in terms of its components or constituent parts may be thought of as reductionist. A useful definition, which is consistent with this broader view, is that of Rose *et al.* (1984), for whom reductionism is:

'the name given to a set of general methods and modes of explanation both of the world of physical objects and of human societies. Broadly, reductionists try to explain the properties of complex wholes – molecules, say, or societies – in terms of the units of which those molecules or societies are composed'.

EXERCISE 10

There are many examples of psychological theories and concepts which fit either or both of Garnham's and Rose *et al.*'s definitions. These can be found in all areas of psychology, but below are a few of the more 'obvious' examples. For each one, try to explain (a) *why* the theory or concept is reductionist, and (b) what are the strengths and/or weaknesses of such an approach.

 i According to *structuralism* (e.g. Wundt), perception is simply a series of sensations (see Chapter 4).
 ii According to Watson's *peripheralism*, thought consists of tiny movements of the vocal chords.
 iii Intelligence is a person's performance on a standardised intelligence test (his or her IQ score).
 iv Psychological sex differences are caused by biological factors (such as hormones).
 v According to Freud, personality development involves progress through a series of *psychosexual* stages.
 vi Schizophrenia is caused by an excess of the neurotransmitter, dopamine.

vii According to Adorno *et al.*, anti-semitism (and other forms of racism) are symptomatic of the *authoritarian personality*.

The mind–body problem: what is the relationship between mind and brain?

Perhaps the oldest and most frequently debated example of reductionism is the mind–body problem (or the problem of mind and brain). Originally a philosophical issue, it continues to be discussed, often passionately, by neurophysiologists, biologists, neuropsychologists and psychologists in general.

Whilst it is generally agreed that the mind (or consciousness) is a property of human beings (as is walking upright on two legs), and that without the human brain there would be no consciousness, a 'problem' remains.

Box 2.7 *The problem of the mind–brain relationship*

- How can two 'things' be related when one of them is physical (the brain has size, weight, shape, density, exists in space and time) and the other apparently lacks all these characteristics?
- How can something that is non-physical/non-material (the mind) influence or produce changes in something that is physical (the brain/body)?

The 'classic' example given by philosophers to illustrate the problem is the act of deciding to lift one's arm. (This example also illustrates the exercise of [free] will: see text.) From a strictly scientific perspective, this kind of causation should be impossible, and science (including psychology and neurophysiology) has traditionally rejected any brand of *philosophical dualism*, that is, the belief in the existence of two essentially different kinds of 'substance', the physical body and the non-physical mind (see Table 2.8).

From an evolutionary perspective, could consciousness have equipped human beings with survival value *unless* it had causal properties (Gregory, 1981), that is, unless it could actually bring about changes in behaviour? Our subjective experiences tell us that our minds *do* affect behaviour and that consciousness does have causal properties (just try lifting your arm). However, many philosophers and scientists from various disciplines have not always shared the layperson's common sense understanding.

Whilst there are many theories of the mind–brain relationship, most are not strictly relevant to the debate about reductionism. Box 2.8 and Figure 2.1 summarise most of the major theories, but emphasis will be given to reductionist approaches, especially as they impinge on *psychological* theories.

Box 2.8 *Some major theories of the mind–brain relationship*

- Theories fall into two main categories: *dualism* (which distinguishes between mind and brain), and *monism* (which claims that only mind or matter is real).

- According to Descartes' seventeenth century dualist theory (which first introduced the mind–body problem into philosophy), the mind can influence the brain, but not vice versa. Whilst *epiphenomenology* sees the mind as a kind of by-product of the brain (the mind has no influence on the brain), *interactionism* sees the influence as two-way.

- *Psychophysical parallelists* are dualists who believe that there is no mind–brain interaction at all: mental and neural events are merely perfectly synchronised or correlated.

- According to *mentalism/idealism*, only mental phenomena are real. *Phenomenological* theories, such as that of Rogers, and *constructionist* explanations of behaviour, have a mentalist 'flavour'.

- Most monist theories take one or other form of *materialism*.

- The *peripheralist* version of materialism is illustrated by Skinner's radical behaviourism (see Chapter 1, pages 16–18). During the 1930s, Skinner denied the existence of mental phenomena (as Watson, the founder of behaviourism, had done). However, from 1945 he began to adopt a less extreme view, recognising their existence, but defining them as *covert/internal actions*, subject to the same laws as overt behavioural events (those of conditioning). This is a form of reductionism.

- *Centralist materialism* (or *mind–brain identity theory*) identifies mental processes with purely physical processes in the central nervous system. Whilst it is logically possible that there might be

---

separate, mental, non-physical phenomena, it just turns out that, as a matter of fact, mental states are identical with physical states of the brain. We are, simply, very complicated physico-chemical mechanisms.

● *Eliminative materialism* represents an extreme reductionist form of (centralist) materialism: see text.

(Based on Flanagan, 1984; Gross, 1995, and Teichman, 1988)

EXERCISE 11

Using your knowledge of biopsychology, try to relate the examples below to the theories outlined in Box 2.8 and Figure 2.1. Specifically, do these examples involve interactions between mind and brain, and, if so, in what direction is the influence taking place?

a The effects of psychoactive drugs.
b Electrical stimulation of the brain.
c Sperry's study of split-brain patients.
d Stress.

Reductionist theories of the mind–brain relationship

As Box 2.8 shows, *eliminative materialism* is an extreme form of reductionist materialism. What makes it reductionist is the attempt to *replace* a psychological account of behaviour with an account in terms of neurophysiology. An example of this approach is Crick's (1994) *The Astonishing Hypothesis: The Scientific Search for the Soul*. According to Crick:

'You, your joys and your sorrows, your memories and your ambitions, your sense of personality and free will, are in fact no more than the behaviour of a vast assembly of nerve cells and their associated molecules'.

But is this a valid equation to make? According to Smith (1994), the mind and brain problem is radically different from other cases of *contingent identity* (identical as a matter of fact) with which it is usually compared, such as 'a gene is a section of the DNA molecule'. What is different is reductionism and the related issue of exactly what is meant by *identity*.

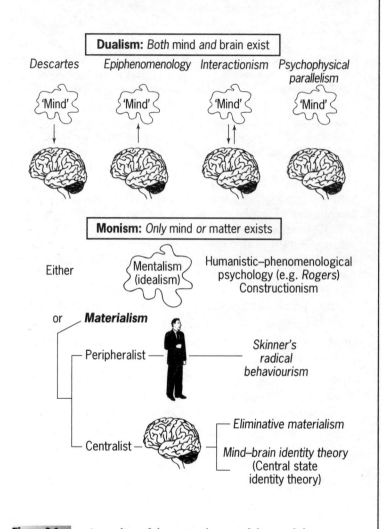

Figure 2.1 *An outline of the major theories of the mind–brain relationship*

> **Box 2.9** *Different meanings of 'identity' relevant to the mind–brain relationship*
>
> Whilst it is generally agreed that we cannot have a mind without a brain, mind states and brain states are not systematically correlated, and the neurophysiological and neurological evidence points towards *token identity*. For example, we cannot just assume that the same neurophysiological mechanisms will be used by two different people both engaged in the 'same' activity of reading (Broadbent, 1981). There are many ways that 'the brain' can perform the same task.
>
> But it is precisely this kind of systematic correlation that mind–brain identity has been taken to imply, whereby whenever a mind state of a certain type occurs, a brain state of a certain type occurs (*type identity*). Token identity means that there must always be a place for an autonomous psychological account of human thought and action.
>
> (Based on Harré *et al.*, 1985)

According to Penrose (1990), there is a built-in indeterminacy in the way that individual neurons and their synaptic connections work (their responses are inherently unpredictable). Yet, despite this unpredictability at the level of the individual units or components, the system as a whole is predictable. The 'nervous system' (or sub-systems within it) does not operate randomly, but in a highly organised, structured way.

Consciousness, intelligence, and memory are properties of the brain as a system, *not* properties of the individual units, and they could not possibly be predicted from analysing the units. Instead, they 'emerge' from interactions between the units that compose the system (and so are called *emergent properties*). The whole is greater than the sum of its parts. (see Box 1.1, page 3.)

Can you be a materialist without being a reductionist?

According to Rose (1992):

'the mind is never replaced by the brain. Instead we have two distinct and legitimate languages, each describing the same unitary phenomena of the material world'.

Rose speaks as a materialist and an *anti-reductionist*, who believes that we should learn how to translate between mind language and brain language (although this may be impossibly difficult). Whilst most materialists are also reductionists, and vice versa, this is not necessarily so. Freud, for example, was a materialist who believed that no single scientific vocabulary (such as anatomy) could adequately describe (let alone explain) all facets of the material world. He believed in the *autonomy of psychological explanation*.

The fact that there are different 'languages' for describing minds and brains (or different *levels of description* or *universes of discourse*) relates to the question of the relevance of knowing, say, what is going on inside our brains when we think or are aware. For Eiser (1994):

'The firing of neurons stands to thought in the same relation as my walking across the room (etc.) stands to my getting some coffee. It is absolutely essential in a causal or physical sense, and absolutely superfluous ... to the logic of the higher-order description. In short, I can accept that it happens, and then happily ignore it'.

This explains how it is possible to be simultaneously a materialist (the brain is necessarily implicated in everything we do and the mind does not represent a different kind of reality) *and* an anti-reductionist (we can describe and explain our thinking without having to 'bring my brain into it'). Two separate levels of description are involved.

Conclusions

Given psychology's intellectual and historical roots in philosophy and natural science, it is hardly surprising that psychological theories have contributed to the debate about free will versus determinism, and reductionism. The possession of free will is a fundamental aspect of our common sense concept of a person. Therefore, any theory calling itself psychological must have something to say about this issue. Equally, belief (or not) in the independence of psychological from neurophysiological explanations of behaviour, is crucial to the survival of psychology itself as a separate discipline. This chapter has tried to capture some of the essential features of both these issues.

Summary

- Our intuitive belief in free will conflicts with the scientific belief in determinism. Determinism also implies behaviour's complete predictability and that everything (including thoughts and behaviour) has a cause. Whilst free will implies having a mind, the things we do with our minds may themselves be determined, despite appearing to be freely chosen.

- Free will is an ambiguous concept and can denote having a choice, not being coerced or constrained, voluntary (as opposed to reflex), and deliberate control (as opposed to automatic information processing). The more automatic our behaviours, the weaker our subjective experience of freedom becomes.

- Penfield demonstrated that voluntarily moving one's limbs involves a different **subjective experience** compared with brain stimulation causing one's limbs to move. This supports the view that free will is part of our experience of being a person, which is demonstrated by **psychological reactance**. Similar to this need to feel free from others' control is **intrinsic motivation/self-determination**.

- Definitions of abnormality, and the diagnosis and treatment of mental disorders, often involve judgements about free will. Temporary or permanent loss of control is a legally acceptable defence in criminal cases, as in the **diminished responsibility** defence (for murder). Legal and moral responsibility presuppose free will.

- For James, a conflict exists between science's belief in determinism and belief in free will as required by other social institutions. He proposed that psychology as a science could only progress by assuming determinism, but belief in free will could be maintained in other contexts. James also distinguished between **soft** and **hard determinism**, the former allowing **conscious mental life** to be the immediate cause of behaviour.

- Freud extended the law of determinism to mental phenomena (**psychic determinism**). Ironically, 'free' association was used in psychoanalysis to reveal the **unconscious causes** of behaviour, our ignorance of which creates an **illusion** of freedom.

- However, Freud recognised the occurrence of 'true' accidents, and argued that therapy enables people to change in limited ways. His concept of **overdetermination** allows the **conscious** mind a role in influencing behaviour, and he often tried to interpret the **meaning** of patients' thoughts and behaviours (rather than look for causes).

- Skinner's radical behaviourism involves a rejection of **explanatory fictions**, such as free will and other mentalistic terms. The illusion of free will survives because the environmental causes of behaviour are often hidden from us. He advocated that negative reinforcement and punishment should be abandoned as means of social control, with only positive reinforcement being used for socialised, civilised behaviour.

- Skinner rejects the notion of 'autonomous man' and removes morality from human behaviour by equating 'good' and 'bad' with what is rewarded and punished respectively. One consequence of this is the **behaviour therapist's dilemma**.

- Rogers stressed self-actualisation, psychological growth and the freedom to choose. The need to understand people's self-concept is central to his **client-centred therapy**, which enables people to change and become more free.

- However, whilst remaining optimistic about 'human nature', Rogers argued that science shows people to be complex machines and not free. The fully functioning person chooses to act the way he or she must.

- Originating in biology, **reductionism** became part of science in general. Although its supporters see reductionism's ultimate aim as accounting for all phenomena (including psychological) in terms of microphysics, any attempt to explain something in terms of its components is reductionist. A long-debated example is the **mind–body problem**.

- Whilst it is generally agreed that a brain is necessary for consciousness, the problem remains of how the non-physical mind can influence the physical brain. From a strictly scientific perspective, such influence should be impossible. However, from an evolutionary perspective, consciousness should be able to produce behaviour change, which is what our subjective experience tells us.

- Theories of the mind–brain relationship are either **dualist** or **monist**. Dualist theories include Descartes' original dualism, epiphenomenology, interactionism, and psychophysical parallelism. Monist theories include mentalism/idealism, **peripheralist materialism** (such as Skinner's radical behaviourism) and **centralist materialism/mind–brain identity theory**.

- Skinner's definition of mental phenomena as **covert/internal actions** is reductionist, as is **eliminative materialism**, which attempts to **replace** psychological accounts of behaviour with neurophysiological ones. The latter confuses **type identity** with **token identity**.

- Whilst individual neurons and their synaptic connections are unpredictable, the nervous system overall is highly organised. **Emergent properties** (such as intelligence and consciousness) reflect the activity of the brain as a system and could not possibly be predicted from analysis of its components.

- Whilst most materialists are also reductionists, some argue that psychology and neurophysiology constitute distinct **levels of description/universes of discourse**, which cannot replace each other. Freud, for example, believed in the **autonomy of psychological explanation**.

CONTROVERSIAL APPLICATIONS

Introduction and overview

3

Whilst all scientific knowledge can be abused or used in controversial ways, psychology is, perhaps, especially open to such abuse. Since its subject matter includes human beings, people's lives are likely to be influenced, directly or indirectly, by what psychologists believe about human behaviour and cognitive processes.

Sometimes this influence is passive, in the sense that people may come to think about themselves differently (and hence act differently) simply by knowing something about a particular theory (such as Freud's psychoanalytic theory: see Chapter 1). More controversially, the influence can be active, as when psychologists (or others) use theories and research findings to deliberately *change* people's attitudes and behaviours (as in advertising), or when individuals' performances on psychometric tests (such as intelligence tests) can determine educational and occupational opportunities.

This chapter considers some of the most controversial applications of psychological theory and research, in particular advertising, propaganda and warfare, and psychometric testing (with an emphasis on intelligence and personality testing). A common thread linking the first three is *persuasion*, which is one form of social influence (see Figure 3.1, page 64).

Social influence, behaviour change and ethics

Having identified the concept of *change* as essential for trying to understand what is controversial about these applications, it is necessary to distinguish between different kinds of change and different kinds of influence. Much of social psychology is concerned with *social influence*, but most of this is not considered controversial, since it is seen as an inevitable feature of social inter-action. It only becomes controversial when psychologists apply their knowledge to influence those who do not share it ('the general public') in ways that are not necessarily in the latter's best interests.

Not knowing that you are being influenced is dubious enough, but changing your behaviour in ways you may not have chosen to makes the influence even more unethical. This has some parallels with participants in field experiments, who not only cannot give their informed consent, but cannot give any consent at all, since they do not realise that there is an experiment taking place! Hence, 'controversial' in this context really means 'ethically dubious'.

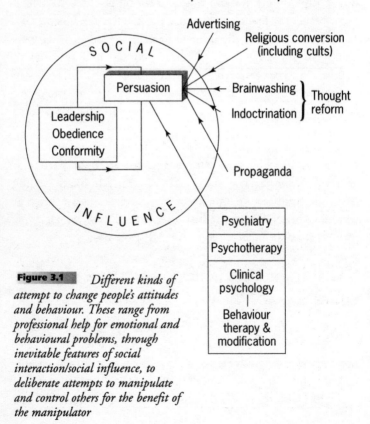

Figure 3.1 *Different kinds of attempt to change people's attitudes and behaviour. These range from professional help for emotional and behavioural problems, through inevitable features of social interaction/social influence, to deliberate attempts to manipulate and control others for the benefit of the manipulator*

The ethics of attitude and behaviour change also apply to clinical psychology, psychotherapy and psychiatry (see Chapter 1). Controversies still arise even when people voluntarily seek help from one or other of these professions. These, and other ethical issues, are discussed in Chapter 6.

Psychology, propaganda and warfare

Psychology and war

According to Richards (1996a), war presents psychology with a dilemma. Since the vast majority of modern psychologists accept that war is an evil pathology, their task should, apparently, be to diagnose its psychological roots. However, such principled opposition is offset by the fact that most psychologists, no less than anyone else, usually feel bound to support the war efforts of their host societies.

Psychologists have increasingly been called upon to use their professional skills in such tasks as selection and training, propaganda and the design of military technology. Psychology (like other disciplines) has been happy to exploit the abundant scientific funding and research opportunities that war provides, which Richards (1996a) believes does not imply cynicism since, in the final analysis, psychologists' own fundamental identifications are generally with their countries' national war aims.

Beginning with the First World War (1914–18), psychology has been shaped, to a significant degree, by its wartime roles. Some of the best known and influential theories and research areas have been stimulated, directly or indirectly, by these roles.

EXERCISE 1

Before reading Box 3.1, try to think of theories and areas of research that you have previously read about and/or discussed which are in some way linked to war. These examples are most likely to be found in the cognitive and social sections of the syllabus.

Box 3.1 *Psychological theory and research stimulated by war*

- Gibson's (1950) *theory of (direct) perception* arose from his research during the Second World War (1939–45), when he was asked by the US Army Air Force to prepare training films that would describe the problems pilots experience when taking off and landing.

- The *intelligence tests* introduced in America for army recruits during the First World War (the army alpha and beta tests) by Yerkes, Goddard and Terman, represented the beginning of mass intelligence testing. Colonel Yerkes supervised the testing of no fewer than 1.75 million recruits (Gould, 1981).

- American psychologists (and sociologists) initially studied *persuasion/persuasive communication* out of concern about the influence on the individual (seen as an isolated being in a 'mass society') of the mass media (as instruments of totalitarian European regimes). However, the American government was also interested in knowing how the media could be used more effectively in advertising, politics, and putting across its policies (especially during the Second World War). The long-term Yale research programme on communications was a direct descendent of the research branch of the US War Department's Information and Education Division. Hovland, who headed the Yale programme, started his experimental work whilst employed by the US War Department, where he was concerned with the practical problems of briefing American military personnel (Brown, 1985).

- Milgram's obedience studies were originally intended to test the view, popular with historians, that Hitler could not have put into operation his plan to systematically destroy millions of Jews and others, without the co-operation of an abnormally obedient German nation.

- Since the First World War, psychologists have become involved in the treatment of those suffering war-related mental disturbances, primarily military personnel traumatised by combat, victims of 'shell shock' (First World War) or 'combat fatigue' (Second World War). These categories were created by psychologists undertaking this work (Richards, 1996a). These categories have been replaced by (and fall within) the more general 'post-traumatic stress disorder' (PTSD). One of the most intensively studied groups of people with PTSD are combat veterans from the

> Vietnam War. Of 2.8 million Vietnam-era veterans who served in combat, 0.5–1.2 million may suffer from PTSD (Wilson *et al.*, 1996)
>
> ● Eysenck's identification of *introversion–extroversion* and *neuroticism–stability* as universal dimensions of human personality occurred whilst he was treating Second World War soldiers at the Mill Hill Emergency Hospital in London (see Gross, 1996).
>
> ● According to Brown (1985), the use of 'thought reform' ('brainwashing' plus indoctrination) by Chinese Communists against Allied prisoners of war (PoWs) during the Korean War (1950–53) caused great anxiety in the West, and raised questions about the nature of loyalty and treason and the preparation of soldiers for captivity. Returning PoWs were extensively studied by the military, psychologists and psychiatrists in several countries and considerable research was undertaken, often financed by military authorities. This included Hebb's (1952) studies of sensory deprivation and sleep deprivation for the Defence Research Board in Canada, and Zimbardo *et al.*'s (1973) prison simulation experiment for the US Office of Naval Research. From such research, lessons were learned as to how to resist indoctrination and the stresses of captivity (Brown, 1985). These techniques of thought reform mirror those used by past and present religious groups, and so-called 'cults'.

The examples given in Box 3.1 represent one basic kind of involvement of psychology with war (Richards, 1996a). By the Second World War, a sub-discipline called 'military psychology' had emerged in the US, concerned with applying psychology for military purposes. According to Geuter (1992), the demands of *Wehrmacht* (armed forces) psychology in the 1930s was crucial in professionalising German psychology, as were the 1917–18 army IQ tests for American psychology (see Box 3.1).

A different kind of involvement took the form of trying to diagnose the psychological roots of war (Richards, 1996a). Freud (1920, 1923) came to see aggression as a separate instinct from sexuality following the horrific carnage of the First World War. He distinguished between the life instinct (or *Eros*), which included sexuality, and the death instinct (or *Thanatos*). Another theory of aggression that has much in common with Freud's is Lorenz's (1966) *ethological* theory.

EXERCISE 2

Try to identify some of the similarites and differences between Freud's and Lorenz's theories of aggression. How valid is it to regard war as simply a form of instinctive aggression? In answering the second question, try to use the concept of *reductionism* (see Chapter 2, pages 52–59).

This kind of involvement of psychology with war has, more recently, taken the form of research into the psychological aspects of the effects of nuclear weapon development during the mid-1980s Cold War. In fact, there is a much longer history of psychological study of the effects of war, especially on children.

Box 3.2 *Some research findings concerning the effects of war on children*

- Several early reports dealt with children's adjustment during World War II, but their findings were inconsistent. Some researchers concluded that children who experienced air raids generally suffered minimal psychological effects (Freud & Burlingham, 1942), whilst others described both acute and chronic post-traumatic stress reactions (Dunsdon, 1941).
- Reports on British children evacuated from cities to the countryside pointed to certain consistent effects, such as impaired concentration, anxiety and delinquency (Dunsdon, 1941; Burt, 1943).
- Significant increases in anxiety were also found in Israeli children following the Yom Kippur War in 1973, the greatest increases occurring in those children who had the lowest levels of peace time anxiety (Milgram & Milgram, 1976). Interestingly, Israeli children living in border communities exposed to shelling over prolonged periods showed no more anxiety than those in communities that were never under fire (Ziv & Israeli, 1973). This was possibly because of the cohesiveness and social support provided in the former, and also the fact that the experience of being shelled had become a part of the children's way of life (Udwin, 1993). However, the adaptation that allows effective

---

functioning in a combat situation may be *maladaptive* under peaceful conditions (Newman *et al.*, 1997).

- Working for UNICEF's psychosocial support programme for children and families in Mostar, Bosnia in 1994, Udwin (1995) identified significant psychological difficulties in many of the 6000 children studied. These included high levels of anxiety, sleeping and concentration problems, depression, withdrawal and behavioural difficulties. Increasingly, children and other civilians are innocent victims, representing a change in twentieth century warfare compared with earlier periods.

(Based on Ladd & Cairns, 1996)

Propaganda and war

'Propaganda' comes from the Latin 'propagare', which refers to the gardener's practice of pinning the fresh shoots of a plant into the earth in order to reproduce new plants which will later take on lives of their own. So, one implication of the term (as originally used in the seventeenth century) is the spread of ideas through their deliberate cultivation or artificial generation.

However, in the twentieth century, propaganda implies something sinister, a deliberate attempt to manipulate, often by concealed or underhand means, the minds of other people for ulterior ends (Brown, 1963). Whilst this change can be dated from the official use of propaganda as a weapon in the total warfare of modern times, beginning with World War I, this was itself an effect of changes in the nature of communication within technically advanced societies. Pratkanis & Aronson (1991) define propaganda as:

'mass suggestion or influence, through the manipulation of symbols and the psychology of the individual. Propaganda is the communication of a point of view with the ulterior goal of having the recipient of the appeal come to 'voluntarily' accept this position as if it were his or her own'.

The aims of propaganda

According to Brown (1963), the chief aims of wartime propaganda are the same regardless of the particular war or the media used (such as pamphlets, leaflets, newspapers, posters, films and public speeches during World War I). These aims were:

- to mobilise and direct hatred against the enemy and undermine the enemy's morale;
- to convince the home public of the rightness of the Allied cause and to increase and maintain fighting spirit;
- to develop the friendship of neutrals and strengthen in their minds the belief that not only were the Allies in the right but they would be victorious in the end and, if possible, to enlist their active support and co-operation;
- to promote a picture of the enemy (as brutal, committing atrocities, wholly responsible for the war in the first place and so on) that justifies the entry of a (usually) peaceable nation into war to '... clear the conscience of the whole nation ...' (Brown, 1963);
- to develop and strengthen the friendship of the Allies;
- to build up strong in-group attitudes and feelings and opposed feelings of hatred towards the enemy as a dangerous out-group. As Brown (1963) claims:

'There is nothing like a war for breaking down class and other barriers and creating feelings of friendship and co-operation within a country because all its previously inwardly-directed aggression and resentment comes to be directed against an external enemy, and it is only in the last stages of a losing effort or after a war has been won that disunity begins to show itself once more'.

EXERCISE 3

How does Brown's quote relate to Tajfel's social identity theory as an explanation of prejudice and discrimination, and to Allport's advocacy of equal status contact and the pursuit of common goals as means of reducing them?

If freedom of choice presupposes a full appreciation of all the alternatives involved, then a feature of propaganda is that it tries to limit our choices deliberately.

Box 3.3 *Some specific techniques used in propaganda*

The use of stereotypes: The Nazi portrayal of Jews (as shown below) is a good illustration of how a generalised belief about an entire group of people is exaggerated in the form of a caricatured portrayal of that group – the negative characteristics are taken to an extreme form.

The substitution of names: Favourable or unfavourable names, with emotional connotations, are substituted for neutral ones. For example, 'Red' (Communist or Russian), 'Union bosses' (presidents of trade unions), 'Huns'/'Krauts' (Germans), and 'Yids' (Jews). Conversely, 'free enterprise' sounds better than 'capitalism'.

Selection: From a mass of complex facts, selection is made for propaganda purposes. Censorship is one way of achieving this and so is a form of propaganda.

Repetition: If a statement or slogan is repeated often enough, it will eventually come to be accepted by the audience, such as Hitler's 'Ein Volk, ein Reich, ein Führer' ('One People, one Empire, one Leader'). During the First World War, there were demands for 'A War to End War' and to 'Make the World Safe for Democracy'.

Assertion: Instead of argument, bald assertions are used to support the propagandist's case, as in the presentation of only one side of the picture, and the deliberate limitation of free thought and questioning.

Pinpointing the enemy: It is useful to present a message not only *for* something but also *against* some real or imagined enemy who is supposedly frustrating the audience's will. This is demonstrated by the Nazi campaign against the Jews (the scapegoats for Germany's humiliation and economic hardships following World War II, which pervaded every aspect of German life in the 1930s. An example of this is the beer mat with the inscription 'Whoever buys from a Jew is a traitor to his people'. (The caricatured face also illustrates the use of stereotypes – see above.)

Appeal to authority: This may be a religious or political figure, science and the professions (also used widely in advertising) or 'the crowd' (the 'band wagon effect'). (Based on Brown, 1963)

Propaganda versus education

Although public health campaigns (such as those for safe sex, and anti-drink-driving) fit Pratkanis and Aronson's definition of propaganda, they are not usually what we have in mind when we use the term, probably because they are aimed at *benefiting* the audience. Similarly, education is often contrasted with propaganda. The former aims to encourage independence of judgement, individual responsibility and an open mind, as well as *how* to think. The latter provides ready-made judgements for the un-thinking, promotes a closed mind and tells people *what* to think.

However, what about the vast majority of high-school textbooks in USA history that virtually ignore the contributions of blacks and other minorities 'to the US scene' (Aronson, 1992)? Such books may not be merely imparting knowledge. This parallels the view that psychology discovers 'facts' about human behaviour which exist objectively (see Chapters 4 and 5). Box 3.4 describes a recent demonstration of 'history as doctrine'.

Box 3.4   *Changing the history of war*

In 1997, a history professor in Japan won a 32-year fight to expose one of the darkest chapters in his country's wartime history. Saburo Ienaga won a Supreme Court ruling that censorship of references in his books to a germ warfare group (Unit 731) were 'unlawful'. Unit 731 conducted biological warfare experiments, including injecting prisoners with anthrax and cholera, exposing them to sub-zero temperatures, and manufacturing bubonic plague bombs (the latter killing thousands of Chinese civilians). None of the 3000 Chinese, Korean, Russian and Mongolian prisoners survived, many being dismembered alive to monitor the progress of the diseases through their bodies.

The Japanese government has never acknowledged these activities, let alone apologised for them. In August, 1997, the Supreme Court in Tokyo ruled that the Japanese education ministry acted illegally when it censored a proposed textbook by Mr Ienaga, but it upheld its right to continue screening all textbooks and removing anything it finds objectionable, including references to war crimes. (From *The Daily Mail*, August 30, 1997)

Advertising

An interesting link between psychology and advertising comes in the form of Watson, the founder of behaviourism (see Chapters 1 and 5). After leaving his academic position at Johns Hopkins University, Watson joined the J. Walter Thompson advertising agency, becoming one of the first and most successful applied psychologists (Banyard & Hayes, 1994).

Scott (1909, cited in Brown, 1963) wrote the first textbook published in Britain on advertising. In it, he identified several principles, the most fundamental being *association*. Not until the late 1930s did advertisers discover Freud – but little came of it until the late 1940s and early 1950s (Brown, 1963).

EXERCISE 4

Taking some advertisments with which you are familiar, try to identify the way that (a) *association* (as demonstrated by classical conditioning), and (b) aspects of Freud's psychoanalytic theory are used. Are these 'techniques' more likely to influence (following Banyard, 1996):

- developing a need (convincing people that they want or need the product);
- noticing the product;
- purchasing the product;
- behaviour after the purchase (encouraging repeat purchases)?

Subliminal advertising

This is by far the most controversial aspect of advertising. It originated with Jim Vicary, an American market researcher, who arranged with the owner of a New Jersey cinema to install a second special projector which, during a film, flashed on the screen phrases such as 'Hungry? Eat Popcorn' and 'Drink Coca-Cola'. These were either flashed so quickly or printed so faintly that they could not be consciously perceived ('subliminal perception' means perception *without* awareness), even after a warning that they were about to appear.

Films treated in this way were alternated with untreated ones throughout the summer of 1956. In the former, sales of popcorn rose by about 50 per cent and soft-drinks by about 18 per cent. Although Vicary himself believed it unlikely that a subliminal stimulus could produce any response at all unless prospective customers already intended buying the product, subliminal advertising caused a storm of protest in the American press, and, later on, in the UK too.

Seeking to scare, rather than sell, a movie producer used a similar technique to Vicary's to flash pictures of a skull and the word 'blood' at key points in pairs of horror movies (Packard, 1957). Despite subliminal messages being legally outlawed (even before it was established whether they really worked), they made a comeback in the mid-1970s. In *The Exorcist* (1974), for example, a death mask was flashed on to the screen subliminally and, more recently, in order to reduce theft, several department stores in America began mixing barely audible and rapidly repeated whispers (such as 'I am honest. I will not steal') with their piped music. Many stores reported dramatic decreases in shoplifting. Also, audio cassette tapes are readily available which supposedly cure stress with soothing sub-audible messages covered by mood music or the ambient sounds of nature (Zimbardo & Leippe, 1991).

More recently still, in 1990, the heavy-metal band Judas Priest went on trial for causing the suicides of two young fans through, allegedly, recording the subliminal message 'Do it' in one of their tracks. They won their case on the grounds that there is no scientific evidence that subliminal messages, even if perceived, could produce such extreme behaviour. It was *this* aspect of the trial which the media emphasised, rather than details of the troubled lives of the two young people concerned (Wadeley, 1996).

Box 3.5 *Are subliminal messages effective?*

To be effective, subliminal stimuli:
- must be able to influence judgements when superimposed on consciously attended-to material. Subliminals *can* have an impact, even when presented simultaneously with something that dominates conscious attention (Greenwald *et al.*, 1989);
- must affect general reactions (so that in the popcorn/Coca-Cola example, Vicary did not want the audience to *like* the words 'Hungry? Eat Popcorn' more than they did before, but to have an increased desire to eat popcorn that would lead to buying more). Subliminal priming studies (e.g. Bargh & Pietromonaco, 1982) show that evaluations of *other* stimuli are influenced by subliminal ones;
- need to be strong and persistent enough to affect the mental processes that lead to subsequent directed behaviour. There is little relevant evidence.

Subliminal *sounds* are less likely to be effective than visual messages, since they are apt to go *totally* unregistered if attention is given to other sounds. According to Pratkanis *et al.* (1990), subliminal 'self-help' tapes have little, if any, therapeutic effect (not even a potentially beneficial placebo effect).

According to Zimbardo & Leippe (1991):

'so far none of the more fabulous claims for subliminals have been borne out by well-controlled and replicable studies. And while some of the touted subliminal techniques merit scientific study, others are simply not possible given what is known about the functioning of the human mind'.

Are subliminal messages ethically unacceptable?

EXERCISE 5

Before reading on, try to identify some of the ethical objections to any form of subliminal advertising. How relevant is the evidence presented in Box 3.5 to the question of ethics?

As noted earlier, exposure of subliminal advertising in the 1950s caused great controversy, resulting in its ban in both the UK and the USA. The British Institute of Practitioners in Advertising published a booklet (*Subliminal Communication*, 1958, cited in Brown, 1963) and banned all its 243 affiliated agencies from using it:

'The free choice by the public to accept or reject is an integral part of all forms of professionally accepted advertising and does not appear to be available to recipients of subliminal communication'.

Whether subliminal messages are unethical depends on the ethics of social influence and persuasion in general (Zimbardo & Leippe, 1991). It is widely agreed that any technique used to influence others (excluding physical coercion) is unethical if it (a) relies on deception, (b) prohibits exposure to opposing messages ('denial of the other side'), and (c) unfairly prevents efforts to resist it.

As far as (a) is concerned, subliminals are deceptive to the extent that their users keep their use a secret, but, conceivably, they might still be effective even when it is openly announced that they are present. Regarding (b), this does not apply to subliminals (but is relevant for evaluating attempts to indoctrinate people, as used by the Moonies, for example: see above).

It is with regard to (c) that subliminals can be viewed as extremely unethical. We cannot defend against something we do not know about and, by definition, we do not know about subliminals. Unlike other forms of influence, such as the image processing of political candidates, or classical conditioning, we cannot resist the influence of subliminals through being observant and mindful. It is only later on – at the time of behavioural decision – that we may ask ourselves why we feel a certain way:

'If subliminal influence should prove to work outside the laboratory in advertising contexts, it would seem highly unethical to use it – mainly because it deprives people of much of their opportunity to resist it' (Zimbardo & Leippe, 1991).

Psychometric testing

Measurement has always been central to experimental science, but trying to quantify *psychological* phenomena ('psychometric' means 'mental measurement') has always proved problematical (Richards, 1996a).

Box 3.6 *Some problems associated with trying to measure psychological phenomena*

- At a fairly abstract level, and in keeping with other sciences, there is the problem of how something can be measured without being changed. In physics (where the riddle first arose), the answer is unambiguously 'it can't'. The nature of measurement is far less straightforward and logical than traditionally assumed.
- How can psychologists identify overt, publicly measurable 'indices' of essentially inaccessible phenomena such as memory, motivation, the structure of personality, and intelligence (and other *hypothetical constructs*: see Chapter 1)? Psychologists tend to assume that these exist in some objective form, but this assumption is a false and a dangerous one to make (see Chapter 4). A good example of a measure that is obviously historically and culturally embedded is the F(Fascism)-scale of authoritarianism (Adorno *et al.*, 1950).
- Once a measuring instrument exists, we can be misled into inferring that what is being measured has a concrete or objective status (this is called *reification*). This is especially likely to occur when performance using the instrument is expressed as a numerical value (as in an IQ score – see text).

As far as psychometrics in general is concerned, there are two major issues that need to be addressed:

1 *Is the test a good test?* Essentially, this refers to the test's *reliability* (consistency), *validity* (whether it measures what it claims to measure), *discriminatory power* (its ability to produce a wide distribution of scores) and *standardisation* (a standardised test is one that has been used with a large, representative sample of the population, which enables individual scores to be compared with appropriate group norms).

2 The above properties are essentially *statistical* and *theoretical* criteria, and a more detailed discussion is beyond the scope of

this chapter. However, even if they were all fulfilled in every case (which they certainly are not), this would have no direct bearing on the *practical* issue, that is, *what is the test being used for* and *how will a person's performance affect his or her educational or occupational future?*

Personality measurement

Kline (1995) identifies three main types of personality test. These are *personality questionnaires and inventories* (the terms are interchangeable), *projective tests* (in which people are presented with ambiguous stimuli, their interpretations of which are taken to reflect unconscious motives), and *objective tests* (in which the test's true purpose is hidden but which provides an objective measurement, such as the circumference of a blown-up balloon as a measure of 'timidity'). There are many examples of each type and each individual test's reliability, validity and so on need to be considered separately.

Box 3.7 *Some advantages of personality questionnaires/inventories compared with other types of personality tests*

- They are easy and quick to use, which is especially important in applied settings. Even the longest (the Minnesota Multiphasic Personality Inventory) only takes about 30 minutes.
- They can be given to many people at the same time, by people without special training in psychology (and the same is true of scoring).
- They can be standardised so as to produce norms, without which individual scores are almost impossible to interpret.
- They can be computerised: all responses to each item are stored in the computer, which simplifies later statistical analysis. Scoring is automatic and error-free, making possible an almost immediate print-out of scores. This can be a great advantage in certain applied settings, such as clinical assessment, vocational guidance, and career counselling.

(Based on Kline, 1995)

The use of personality testing in occupational assessment

The use of personality testing in occupational assessment has been steadily increasing over the past 20 years, with some recent surveys suggesting that up to two-thirds of large organisations in the UK use personality tests for selecting managers (Drakeley, 1997). The vast majority – but not all – use tests responsibly and wisely.

The British Psychological Society has promoted responsible test use by developing the Certificate of Competence in Occupational Testing in order to raise standards. To reach the highest ('Full Level B') standard, those wishing to use personality tests have to demonstrate that they know how to use such instruments for selection, promotion, redundancy, individual personal development, team development, career guidance, and counselling. Of these, promotion and redundancy are especially controversial.

EXERCISE 6

Before reading on, think about *why* the use of personality tests for promotion and redundancy is more controversial than their other uses as listed above.

With promotion and redundancy, the individual is already employed by the organisation. His or her behaviour and 'personality' could be readily observed at work and the normal appraisal system should be sufficient without the use of tests ('Doesn't my track record speak for itself?'). Many employees feel that personality testing is unnecessary and an insensitive intrusion into their private lives (Drakeley, 1997).

Box 3.8 *Arguments for and against the use of personality tests for promotion and redundancy*

The case for
- Tests are patently fairer than many of the flawed, informal procedures (such as favouritism, and the 'old-boy' network) used within some organisations.

- They provide standardised, numerical information allowing easy comparison of people on the same criteria.
- Good tests produce explicit and specific indications of temperament (a 'score') as opposed to vague, ambiguous, coded platitudes (such as 'satisfactory', 'high-flyer') often found in annual appraisals.
- Good tests are 'scientific', that is, they have soundly based theoretical and empirical foundations.

The case against

- Personality measurement usually involves profiling an individual on several 'traits', but these can range from 15 to 30. How many are needed to describe personality with any degree of precision? For any given job, several different combinations of traits could be equally effective.
- A person's performance is likely to be influenced by the situation he or she works in, and often the most salient aspect of the situation is other people. Relatively little is known about the dynamic and complex ways in which different personalities might interact to affect a particular individual's behaviour.

(From Drakeley, 1997)

For the reasons given in Box 3.8, Drakeley believes that personality tests should be used with caution. For example, should tests alone be used for redundancy selection? He concludes that this can only be justified:

'when future job performance cannot reasonably be predicted from current or past job performance. In the particular case of redundancy, this limits the use of such procedures to situations involving real and substantial job redesign'.

The measurement of intelligence

Intelligence (or IQ/Intelligence Quotient) tests form one kind of *ability* test, designed to measure underlying constructs that are not a direct result of training (Coolican, 1996). They are contrasted with *attainment* (or achievement) tests (such as tests of reading and comprehension, spelling and numeracy) designed to assess *specific* information learned in school. *Aptitude* tests form a third kind of test, aimed at measuring *potential* performance (such as a general logic test designed to predict how good someone would be at computer programming). As will be seen, these distinctions are problematical and controversial.

One widely used test is the Wechsler Intelligence Scale for Children (WISC), originally constructed in the USA but now standardised on the UK population (WISC-III UK: Wechsler, 1992). Like Wechsler's tests (which include the Wechsler Adult Intelligence Scale/WAIS), the British Ability Scales (BAS: Elliot *et al.*, 1979, revised 1983) include a battery of verbal and non-verbal tests, and several visual perceptual and cognitive tests.

Through the introduction of a new statistical procedure, the BAS can now be used either as a *criterion-referenced* assessment (indicating whether a child has successfully achieved a given objective or not, irrespective of whether this is appropriate for its age), or as a *norm-referenced* assessment (involving a comparison between an individual's score and the typical score on the test for that individual's age group). Typically, IQ tests are norm-referenced and administered (at least in the case of *individual tests*, such as the WAIS and the BAS) only by those with special training, such as educational psychologists. However, assessment under the National Curriculum, for example, is criterion-referenced, with standard assessment tests (SATs) administered by class teachers.

For and against IQ tests

One argument in favour of the use of IQ assessment is that it has *prevented* some children from being segregated into special schools or classes. Thus, there are cases where a child's IQ score indicates a *higher* level of ability than is reflected in his or her attainments or the teacher's perceptions (Quicke, 1982). This is particularly relevant to areas of learning difficulty which, by definition, relate to a discrepancy between the child's actual cognitive ability (as reflected in the IQ score) and his or her (more limited) specific attainments (Coolican, 1996).

Conversely, Bee (1994) claims that the most important use of IQ tests is in identifying children who might need or benefit from special education. Children whose speed of learning is much faster or slower than normal may be given an IQ test to see if they are gifted or retarded. However, Bee also argues that, whilst it is generally agreed that schools need to diagnose and sort children, what is most controversial about IQ tests is their use as a *central basis* for such sorting.

EXERCISE 7

Before reading on, think about some of the limitations of IQ tests. Is the distinction (made above) between ability and attainment tests valid, and how might this relate to the argument that IQ tests do not measure what they claim to measure?

Box 3.9 *Some arguments against the use of IQ tests*

- IQ tests were designed to measure children's basic capacity or underlying *competence*, whilst achievement/attainment tests are supposed to measure what they have actually learned (*performance*). Each of us presumably has some upper limit of ability (what we could do under ideal conditions, when we are maximally motivated, well and rested). However, everyday conditions are rarely ideal and we typically perform below this hypothetical ability. In fact, it is not *possible* to measure competence and so we are *always* measuring 'today's' performance. According to Bee (1994), logically:

    'all IQ tests are really achievement tests to some degree. The difference between tests called IQ tests and those called achievement tests is really a matter of degree'.

- Whilst IQ scores do become quite stable in late childhood, individual children's IQ scores can and do fluctuate, especially in response to any life stress.

- Traditional tests simply fail to measure a whole host of cognitive and social skills likely to be highly significant for getting on in the world, such as creativity/divergent thinking, insight, 'street smarts', and social intelligence (reading other people's emotional states and social behaviour: Gardner, 1983; Sternberg, 1990). IQ tests, in keeping with why they were originally designed, have an excessively narrow focus on the specific range of skills needed for school success ('school intelligence'), which includes convergent, logical thinking. Intellectual ability is *reduced* to a single (IQ) number (see Chapter 2).

● If IQ score alone is used as a measure of a child's functioning, then a child who is categorised as having learning difficulties (IQ below 70), but who nonetheless has sufficient social skills to function well in a regular classroom, would be inappropriately excluded.

● Knowing a child's IQ score can result in a *self-fulfilling prophecy*. Based on the belief that IQ is a measure of 'true' – and fixed – ability, the child is treated accordingly (such as placement in remedial classes or special schools), which could actually influence its development, including its IQ score.

(Based on Bee, 1994; and Cernovsky, 1997).

Bee (1994) argues that the most serious objection to the use of IQ tests is the fact that they are *biased*, especially against minority groups (see Chapter 5). Taking such tests and doing well may also require certain test-taking skills, motivations and attitudes that are less common especially among African–American children. Despite attempts to eliminate all types of bias:

'When IQ tests are used for diagnosis in schools, proportionately more minority than white children continue to be diagnosed as retarded or slow' (Bee, 1994).

As a result of several lawsuits, there are many places in the USA (such as California) where the use of IQ tests for diagnosis and placement of African–American and other minority children is forbidden.

Conclusions

This chapter has highlighted some of those areas where 'psychological technology' has been (and still is) used – the mass media, international relations, commerce and industry and education – and has discussed how these applications are controversial. Many of the controversies are based on the belief that people are manipulated into behaving in particular ways, their freedom curtailed, or their lives shaped by their performance on tests that claim to measure highly complex aspects of human functioning.

Summary

- Psychology is especially open to abuse because of its subject matter. Active forms of social influence, in which psychologists apply their knowledge to influence people who do not share this knowledge in ways that may not be in their best interests, are controversial and ethically dubious. This also applies to the consequences for people of their performance on psychometric tests.
- Psychology has been shaped, since the First World War, by its wartime roles, which have stimulated many influential theories and areas of research. These include Gibson's theory of perception, the army alpha and beta intelligence tests, persuasive communication, Milgram's obedience studies, and Eysenck's personality tests.
- Attempts to diagnose the psychological roots of war include Freud's distinction between the life and death instincts. There is also a long history of research into the effects of war, especially on children.
- Propaganda was first officially used as a weapon in the First World War. Regardless of which particular communication media are used, wartime propaganda has several aims. These include undermining the enemy's morale, maintaining fighting spirit, promoting a picture of the enemy that justifies involvement in the war, and building strong pro-in-group and anti-out-group feelings.
- Propaganda deliberately tries to limit people's choices, either through presenting one viewpoint and excluding all others (as

in censorship), or through use of caricature, stereotypes, emotive names, repetitive slogans, and the appeal to authority.

- Propaganda is usually contrasted with education, the latter encouraging independent thinking, individual responsibility and an open mind. However, textbooks can be very biased, as in the case of the Japanese government's censorship of school history books for reference to that country's war crimes.

- The first textbook on advertising published in Britain identified **association** as the fundamental principle, and Watson, the founder of behaviourism in America, became one of the first and most successful applied psychologists when he joined a major advertising agency. Advertisers later began using principles derived from Freud's psychoanalytic theory.

- **Subliminal advertising** was originally used in cinemas to increase sales of popcorn and Coca-Cola. Subliminal messages have also been used in other ways, both before and since being made illegal. They can influence judgements when superimposed on consciously-attended to material, and produce general reactions (such as increasing the desire to eat popcorn). However, their influence on behaviour is much less certain. Subliminals remain highly controversial mainly because, unlike other forms of influence, they deprive people of the opportunity to resist them.

- A good **psychometric test** should be reliable, valid, have discriminatory power and be standardised. These statistical and theoretical properties are distinct from what the tests are used for.

- Personality questionnaires/inventories have clear advantages compared with projective and objective tests, including the automatic and error-free scoring useful in applied settings, such as clinical assessment, vocational guidance, and career counselling.

- Personality testing in occupational assessment is increasingly being used by UK organisations, the most controversial uses of such tests being for promotion and redundancy. The only justification for using a test as the sole basis for redundancy selection is when future job performance cannot be predicted from current or past performance.

- Intelligence (IQ) tests are usually defined as **ability** tests, as opposed to **attainment** or **aptitude** tests. The British Ability Scales (BAS) comprise a battery of verbal and non-verbal tests, plus several visual perceptual and cognitive tests. The BAS can be used either as **criterion-referenced** or **norm-referenced**, as **individual** IQ tests typically are.

- IQ assessment can prevent children from being placed in special schools or classes. Conversely, they can identify children who might **benefit** from special education. Although it is generally agreed that schools need to diagnose and sort children, it is controversial to use IQ tests as the basis for doing this.

- Since it is impossible to measure **competence** (as IQ tests claim to do), the difference between competence and **performance** (as measured by attainment tests) is only one of **degree**. Traditional tests fail to measure a variety of cognitive and social skills important for everyday life and are narrowly focused on 'school intelligence'. Also, knowing a child's IQ score can result in a **self-fulfilling prophecy**. Most seriously of all, IQ tests are **biased**, especially against minority groups.

PSYCHOLOGY AS A SCIENCE

Introduction and overview

As was seen in Chapter 1, psychology is commonly defined as the *scientific* study of behaviour and cognitive processes (or mind or experience). In effect, psychology textbooks comprise accounts of how different psychologists have put this definition into practice, through their use of various investigative methods to study a wide variety of behaviours and cognitive processes.

This chapter turns the spotlight once more on that definition of psychology. It does this by examining the nature of science (including the major features of scientific method), and by tracing some of the major developments in psychology's history as a scientific discipline. This enables the question of how appropriate it is to use scientific method to study human behaviour and cognitive processes to be addressed, and the validity of this widely accepted definition to be assessed.

Some philosophical roots of science and psychology

As noted in Chapter 2, Descartes was the first to distinguish formally between mind and matter (*philosophical dualism*), which had an enormous impact on the development of both psychology as a science and science in general. Dualism allowed scientists to treat matter as inert and completely distinct from themselves, which meant that the world could be described *objectively*, without reference to the human observer. Objectivity became the ideal of science, and was extended to the study of human behaviour and social institutions by Comte in the mid-1800s, calling it *positivism*.

Descartes also promoted *mechanism*, the view that the material world comprises objects which are assembled like a huge machine and operated by mechanical laws. He extended this view to living organisms, including, eventually, the human body. Because the mind is non-material, Descartes believed that, unlike the physical world, it can be investigated only through introspection (observing one's own thoughts and feelings). He was also one of the first advocates of *reductionism* (see Chapter 2).

Figure 4.1   *René Descartes (1596–1650)*

Empirism refers to the ideas of the seventeenth and eighteenth century British philosophers, Locke, Hume and Berkeley. They believed that the only source of true knowledge about the world is sensory experience (what comes to us through our senses or what can be inferred about the relationship between such sensory facts.) Empirism is usually contrasted with *nativism* (or *rationalism*), according to which knowledge of the world is largely innate or inborn.

EXERCISE 1

Try to identify examples of psychological theory and research which reflect empirist or nativist views. (Another way of doing this is to ask where in psychology the *nature–nurture* or *heredity* and *environment* debate takes place.)

The word 'empirical' ('through the senses') is often used to mean 'scientific', implying that what scientists do, and what distinguishes them from non-scientists, is carry out experiments and observations as ways of collecting data or 'facts' about the world (hence, 'empirical methods' for 'scientific methods'). *Empiricism* (as distinct from empirism) proved to be one of the central influences on the development of physics and chemistry.

Empiricism and psychology

Prior to the 1870s, there were no laboratories specifically devoted to psychological research, and the early scientific psychologists had trained mainly as physiologists, doctors, philosophers, or some combination of these. The two professors who set up the first two psychological laboratories deserve much of the credit for the development of academic psychology. They were Wundt (1832–1920) in Germany and James (1842–1910) in the USA (Fancher, 1979).

Wundt's contribution

A physiologist by training, Wundt is generally regarded as the 'founder' of the new science of experimental psychology, or what he called 'a new domain of science' (1874). Having worked as Helmholtz's assistant, Wundt eventually became professor of 'scientific philosophy' at Leipzig University in 1875, illustrating the lack of distinct boundaries between the various disciplines which combined to bring about psychology's development (Fancher, 1979).

Figure 4.2 *Wilhelm Wundt (1832–1920)*

In 1879, Wundt converted his 'laboratory' at Leipzig into a 'private institute' of experimental psychology. For the first time, a place had been set aside for the explicit purpose of conducting psychological research, and hence 1879 is widely accepted as the 'birthdate' of psychology as a discipline in its own right. From its modest beginnings, the institute began to attract people from all over the world, who returned to their own countries to establish laboratories modelled on Wundt's.

Box 4.1 *Wundt's study of the conscious mind: introspective psychology and structuralism*

Wundt believed that conscious mental states could be scientifically studied through the systematic manipulation of antecedent variables (those that occur before some other event), and analysed by carefully controlled techniques of introspection. *Introspection* was a rigorous and highly disciplined technique for analysing conscious experience into its most basic elements (*sensations* and *feelings*). Participants were always advanced psychology students who had been carefully trained to introspect properly.

Sensations are the raw sensory content of consciousness, devoid of all 'meaning' or interpretation, and all conscious thoughts, ideas, perceptions and so on were assumed to be combinations of sensations. Based on his experiment in which he listened to a metronome beating at varying rates, Wundt concluded that feelings could be analysed in terms of *pleasantness–unpleasantness*, *tension–relaxation*, and *activity–passivity*.

Wundt believed that introspection made it possible to cut through the learned categories and concepts that define our everyday experience of the world, and so expose the 'building blocks' of experience. Because of introspection's central role, Wundt's early brand of psychology was called *introspective psychology* (or *introspectionism*), and his attempt to analyse consciousness into its elementary sensations and feelings is known as *structuralism*.
(Based on Fancher, 1979)

EXERCISE 2

1 Consider the difficulties that might be involved in relying on introspection to formulate an account of the nature of conscious experience (i.e. an account that applies to people in general).
2 In what ways is structuralism *reductionist*? (see Chapter 2).
3 Which major theory of perception rejects this structuralist approach? Outline its principal features (see Box 1.1, page 3).

James' contribution

James taught anatomy and physiology at Harvard University in 1872, and by 1875 was calling his course *The Relations Between Physiology and Psychology*. In the same year, he established a small laboratory, used mainly for teaching purposes. In 1878, he dropped anatomy and physiology and for several years taught 'pure psychology'.

His view of psychology is summarised in *The Principles of Psychology* (1890), which includes discussion of instinct, brain function, habit, the stream of consciousness, the self, attention, memory, perception, free will (Chapter 2) and emotion.

The Principles provided the famous definition of psychology as 'the Science of Mental Life' (see Chapter 1). Ironically, however, James was very critical both of his book and of what psychology could offer as a science. He became increasingly interested in philosophy and disinterested in psychology, although in 1894 he became the first American to call favourable attention to the recent work of the then little known Viennese neurologist, Sigmund Freud (Fancher, 1979).

Figure 4.3 *William James (1842–1910)*

James proposed a point of view (rather than a theory) that directly inspired *functionalism,* which emphasises behaviour's purpose and utility (Fancher, 1979). Functionalism, in turn, helped to stimulate interest in individual differences, since they determine how well or poorly individuals will adapt to their environments. These attitudes made Americans especially receptive to Darwin's (1859) ideas about individual variation, evolution by natural selection, and the 'survival of the fittest'.

Watson's behaviourist revolution: a new subject matter for psychology

Watson took over the psychology department at Johns Hopkins University in 1909 and immediately began cutting psychology's ties with philosophy and strengthening those with biology. At that time, Wundt's and James's studies of consciousness were still the 'real' psychology, but Watson was doing research on non-humans and became increasingly critical of the use of introspection.

Figure 4.4 *John Broadus Watson (1878–1958)*

In particular, Watson argued that introspective reports were unreliable and difficult to verify. It is impossible to check the accuracy of such reports because they are based on purely private experience, to which the investigator has no possible means of access. As a result, Watson (1913) redefined psychology in his famous 'behaviourist manifesto' of 1913.

Box 4.2 *Watson's (1913) 'behaviourist manifesto'*

Watson's article 'Psychology as the behaviourist views it' is often referred to as the 'behaviourist manifesto', a charter for a truly scientific psychology. It was *behaviourism* which was to represent a rigorous empirist approach within psychology for the first time.

According to Watson:

'Psychology as the behaviourist views it is a purely objective natural science. Its theoretical goal is the prediction and control of behaviour. Introspection forms no essential part of its methods, nor is the scientific value of its data dependent upon the readiness with which they lend themselves to interpretation in terms of consciousness. The behaviourist ... recognises no dividing line between man and brute. The behaviour of a man ... forms only a part of the behaviourist's total scheme of investigation.'

Three features of this 'manifesto' deserve special mention:

- Psychology must be purely objective, excluding all subjective data or interpretations in terms of conscious experience. This redefines psychology as the 'science of behaviour' (rather than the 'science of mental life').

- The goals of psychology should be to predict and control behaviour (as opposed to describing and explaining conscious mental states), a goal later endorsed by Skinner's *radical behaviourism* (see Chapter 1).

- There is no fundamental (*qualitative*) distinction between human and non-human behaviour. If, as Darwin had shown, humans evolved from more simple species, then it follows that human behaviour is simply a more complex form of the behaviour of other species (the difference is merely *quantitative*, one of degree). Consequently, rats, cats, dogs and pigeons became the major source of psychological data: since 'psychological' now meant 'behaviour' rather than 'consciousness', non-humans that were convenient to study, and whose environments could easily be controlled, could replace people as experimental subjects.

(Based on Fancher, 1979, and Watson, 1913)

EXERCISE 3

Try to formulate arguments for and against Watson's claim that there is only a *quantitative* difference between the behaviour of humans and non-humans.

In his 1915 Presidential address to the American Psychological Association, Watson talked about his recent 'discovery' of Pavlov's work on conditioned reflexes in dogs. He proposed that the conditioned reflex could become the foundation for a full-scale human psychology.

The extreme environmentalism of Locke's empirism (see page 88) lent itself well to the behaviourist emphasis on learning (through the process of Pavlovian or classical conditioning). Whilst Locke had described the mind at birth as a *tabula rasa* ('blank slate') on which experience writes, Watson, in rejecting the mind as suitable for a scientific psychology, simply swapped mind for behaviour: it is now behaviour that is shaped by the environment.

According to Miller (1962), empirism provided psychology with both a *methodology* (stressing the role of observation and measurement) and a theory, including analysis into elements (such as stimulus–response units) and *associationism* (which explains how simple elements can be combined to form more complex ones).

Behaviourism also embodied positivism, in particular the emphasis on the need for scientific rigour and objectivity. Humans were now conceptualised and studied as 'natural phenomena', with subjective experience, consciousness and other characteristics (traditionally regarded as distinctive human qualities) no longer having a place in the behaviourist world.

The cognitive revolution

Academic psychology in the USA and the UK was dominated by behaviourism for the next 40 years. However, criticism and dissatisfaction with it culminated in a number of 'events', all taking place in 1956, which, collectively, are referred to as the 'cognitive revolution'.

This new way of thinking about and investigating people was called the *information-processing approach*. At the centre of this is the *computer analogy*, the view that human cognition can be understood by comparing it with the functioning of a digital computer. It was now acceptable to study the mind again, although its conceptualisation was very different from that of Wundt, James and the other pioneers of the 'new psychology' prior to Watson's 'behaviourist revolution'.

Box 4.3 *The 1956 'cognitive revolution'*

- At a meeting at the Massachusetts Institute of Technology (MIT), Chomsky introduced his theory of language. Miller presented a paper on the 'magical number seven' in short-term memory, and Newell and Simon presented a paper on the logical theory machine (or logic theorist), with a further paper by Newell *et al.* (1958), which Newell & Simon (1972) extended into the general problem solver (GPS).

- The first systematic attempt to investigate concept formation (in adults) from a cognitive psychological perspective was reported (Bruner *et al.*, 1956).

- At Dartmouth College, New Hampshire (the 'Dartmouth Conference'), ten academics met to discuss the possibilities of producing computer programs that could 'behave' or 'think' intelligently. These academics included McCarthy (generally attributed with having coined the term 'artificial intelligence'), Minsky, Simon, Newell, Chomsky and Miller.

(Based on Eysenck & Keane, 1995)

Science, scientism and mainstream psychology

Despite this major change in psychology after 1956, certain central assumptions and practices within the discipline have remained essentially the same, and these are referred to as *mainstream psychology*. Harré (1989) refers to the mainstream as the 'old paradigm', which he believes continues to be haunted by certain 'unexamined presuppositions', one of which is *scientism*, defined by Van Langenhove (1995) as:

> 'the borrowing of methods and a characteristic vocabulary from the natural sciences in order to discover causal mechanisms that explain psychological phenomena'.

Scientism maintains that all aspects of human behaviour can and should be studied using the methods of natural science, which claims to be the sole means of establishing 'objective truth'. This can be achieved by studying phenomena removed from any particular context ('context-stripping' exposes them in their 'pure' form), and in a *value-free* way (there is no bias on the investigator's part). The most reliable way of doing this is through the laboratory experiment, the method providing the greatest degree of control over relevant variables (see pages 108–113). As noted above, these beliefs and assumptions add up to the traditional view of science known as positivism.

EXERCISE 4

Try to find examples of experimental studies of human behaviour that fit the definition of 'context-stripping' given above. Probably the 'best' examples will come from social psychology, which in itself should suggest criticisms of this approach to studying behaviour. (See also Chapter 5, pages 119–121.)

Although much research has moved beyond the confines of the laboratory experiment, the same positivist logic is still central to how psychological inquiry is conceived and conducted. Method and measurement still have a privileged status:

'Whether concerned with mind or behaviour (and whether conducted inside or outside the laboratory), research tends to be constructed in terms of the separation (or reduction) of entities into independent and dependent variables and the measurement of hypothesised relationships between them' (Smith *et al.*, 1995).

Despite the fact that since the mid-1970s the natural sciences model has become the subject of vigorous attacks, psychology is still to a large extent dominated by it. The most prominent effect of this is the dominance of experiments (Van Langenhove, 1995). This has far-reaching effects on the way psychology *pictures* people as more or less passive and mechanical information-processing devices, whose behaviour can be split up into variables. It also affects the way psychology *deals* with people. In experiments, people are not treated as single individuals, but as interchangeable 'subjects'. There is no room for individualised observations.

What do we mean by 'science'?

The major features of science

Most psychologists and philosophers of science would probably agree that for a discipline to be called a science, it must possess certain characteristics. These are summarised in Box 4.4 and Figure 4.5.

Box 4.4 *The major features of science*

- **A definable subject matter:** This changed from conscious human thought to human and non-human behaviour, then to cognitive processes within psychology's first 80 years as a separate discipline.
- **Theory construction:** This represents an attempt to explain observed phenomena, such as Watson's attempt to account for (almost all) human and non-human behaviour in terms of classical conditioning, and Skinner's subsequent attempt to do the same with operant conditioning.
- **Hypothesis testing:** This involves making specific predictions about behaviour under certain specified conditions (for example, predicting that by combining the sight of a rat with the sound of a hammer crashing down on a steel bar just behind his head, a small child will learn to fear the rat: see the case of Little Albert, in Gross & McIlveen, 1998).
- **The use of empirical methods:** These are used to collect data (evidence) relevant to the hypothesis being tested.

What is 'scientific method'?

The account given in Box 4.4 and Figure 4.5 of what constitutes a science is non-controversial. However, it fails to tell us how the *scientific process* takes place, the sequence of 'events' involved (such as where the theory comes from in the first place, and how it is related to observation of the subject matter), or the exact relationship between theory construction, hypothesis testing and data collection. (See page 100.)

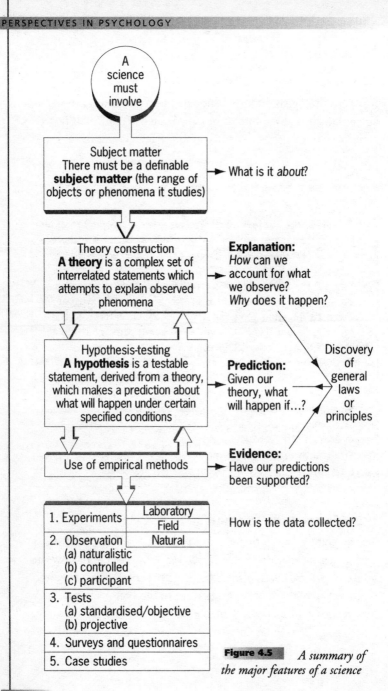

Figure 4.5 *A summary of the major features of a science*

Table 4.1 *Some common beliefs, and alternative views, about 'science' and 'scientific method'*

Common beliefs

- Scientific discovery begins with simple, unbiased, unprejudiced observation (i.e. the scientist simply 'samples' the world without any preconceptions, expectations or predetermined theories).
- From the resulting sensory evidence ('data'/sense-data), generalised statements of fact will take shape (i.e. we gradually build up a picture of what the world is like based on a number of separate 'samples').
- ▲ The essential feature of scientific activity is the use of empirical methods, through which the sensory evidence is gathered (i.e. what distinguishes science from non-science is performing experiments and so on).
- ✦ The truth about the world (the objective nature of things, what the world is 'really like') can be established through properly controlled experiments and other ways of collecting 'facts' (i.e. science can tell us about reality as it is *independently* of the scientist or the activity of observing it).
- ✗ Science involves the steady accumulation of knowledge, so that each generation of scientists adds to the discoveries of previous generations.

Alternative views

- There is no such thing as 'unbiased' or 'unprejudiced' observation. Our observation is always selective, interpretative, pre-structured and directed (i.e. we must have at least some idea of what we are looking for, otherwise we cannot know when we have found it).
- 'Data' do not constitute 'facts': evidence usually implies measurement, numbers, recordings and so on which need to be interpreted in the light of a theory. Facts do not exist objectively and cannot be discovered through 'pure observation'. 'Fact' = Data + Theory (Deese, 1972).
- ▲ Despite the central role of data collection, data alone do not make a science. Theory is just as crucial, because without it, data have no meaning (see second bullet above).
- ✦ Scientific theory and research reflect the biases, prejudices, values and assumptions of the individual scientist, as well as of the scientific community to which he or she belongs. Science is *not* value-free (see text).
- ✗ Science involves an endless succession of long, peaceful periods ('normal science') and 'scientific revolutions' (Kuhn, 1962: see Table 4.3).
- Science has a warm, human, exciting, argumentative, creative 'face' (Collins, 1994: see Box 4.5).

(Based on Medawar, 1963, and Popper, 1972)

Collectively, these 'events' and relationships are referred to as (the) *scientific method*. Table 4.1 (page 99) summarises some common beliefs about both science and scientific method, as identified by Medawar (1963) and Popper (1972), together with some alternative views.

Box 4.5   *The inner world of scientists*

According to Richards & Wolpert (1997), scientists, outside their own habitat, are a poorly understood species. If they feature in popular awareness at all, it is through a limited set of media stereotypes. With a few exceptions, if scientists are not mad or bad, they are perceived as personality-free, their measured tones and formal reports implying ways of thinking and working far removed from the intellectual and emotional messiness of other human activities. Richards and Wolpert engaged in a series of conversations with several eminent scientists (including chemists, immunologists, biologists, biochemists, neuro- and evolutionary biologists) in an attempt to redress the balance, and give a rare glimpse of the human reality of scientific life.

Scientists think and feel about their work using the same psychological apparatus as the rest of us. The human qualities of science come over very strongly: its energy and imaginative richness, the frustration, love and despair which enslaves its practitioners.

For example, Mitchison (an immunologist) says that experiments start with 'the act of creation':

   '... Not all experiments you think of are good experiments, but thinking of one is just wonderful, eureka! It's fantastic'.

According to Edelman (an immunologist and neurobiologist), stumbling upon the solution to a problem when you least expect to find it is a '... remarkable pleasure ...'. Some scientists are like voyeurs, with '... almost a lustful feeling of excitement when a secret of nature is revealed ...'.

(Adapted from Richards & Wolpert, 1997)

As a result of the first two beliefs identified in Table 4.1, Popper (1972) has revised the stages of the scientific process as proposed by the classical view (the *inductive method*). This, together with Popper's revised version, is shown in Table 4.2.

Table 4.2 *Comparison between the classical, inductive view of science and Popper's revised version*

Inductive method	Popper's version
Observation and method	Problem (usually a refutation of an existing theory or prediction)
Inductive generalisation	Proposed solution or new theory
Hypothesis	Deduction of testable statements (hypotheses) from the new theory. This relates to the *hypothetico-deductive method,* which is usually contrasted with/opposed to the inductive method. In practice, both approaches are involved in the scientific process and are complementary.
Attempted verification of hypothesis	Tests or attempts to refute by methods including observation and experiment
Proof or disproof	Establishing a preference between competing theories
Knowledge	

(Based on Popper, 1972)

Can psychology be a science if psychologists cannot agree what psychology is?

As previously noted, definitions of psychology have changed during its lifetime, largely reflecting the influence and contributions of its major theoretical *approaches* or orientations. In this chapter (and Chapter 1) it has been seen that each approach rests upon a different image of what people are like, which in turn determines what is important to study, as well as the methods of study that can and should be used.

EXERCISE 5

What is the underlying image of the person associated with each of the major theoretical approaches within psychology? Which of these do you consider captures your own experience, and your experience of others, most accurately, and why? (You might find it helpful to refer to Chapter 1.)

Consequently, different approaches can be seen as self-contained disciplines, as well as different facets of the same discipline (Kuhn, 1962; Kline, 1988).

Kuhn argues that a field of study can only legitimately be considered a science if a majority of its workers subscribe to a common, global perspective or *paradigm*. According to Kuhn, this means that psychology is *pre-paradigmatic*: it lacks a paradigm, without which it is still in a state (or stage) of *pre-science*. Whether psychology has, or has ever had, a paradigm, is hotly debated (see Table 4.3, page 103.).

Is a theoretical approach the same as a paradigm?

As Table 4.3 shows, Kuhn (a philosopher of science), along with some psychologists, maintains that psychology is still a pre-science. Others believe that psychology has already undergone at least two revolutions, and is in a stage of normal science, with cognitive psychology the current paradigm. A third view, which represents a blend of the first two, is that psychology currently, and simultaneously, has a number of paradigms.

For example, Smith & Cowie (1991) identify psychoanalysis, behaviourism, sociobiology, the information-processing, and cognitive–developmental approaches as paradigms, with the last being the most important as far as child development is concerned. For Davison & Neale (1994) there are 'four major paradigms of contemporary abnormal psychology', namely, the biological, psychoanalytic, learning (behaviourist) and cognitive. (See page 104.)

Table 4.3 *Kuhn's three stages in the development of a science, and some views about how they apply to psychology*

Stages in the development of a science (●) and their application to psychology (■)

- ● *Pre-science*: No paradigm has evolved and there are several schools of thought or theoretical orientations.
- ■ Like Kuhn, Joynson (1980) and Boden (1980) argue that psychology is pre-paradigmatic. Kline (1988) sees its various approaches as involving different paradigms.
- ● *Normal science:* A paradigm has emerged, dictating the kind of research that is carried out and providing a framework for interpreting results. The details of the theory are filled in and workers explore its limits. Disagreements can usually be resolved within the limits allowed by the paradigm.
- ■ According to Valentine (1982), behaviourism comes as close as anything could to a paradigm. It provides: (i) a clear definition of the subject matter (behaviour, as opposed to 'the mind'); (ii) fundamental assumptions, in the form of the central role of learning (especially conditioning), and the analysis of behaviour into stimulus–response units, which allow prediction and control; (iii) a methodology, with the controlled experiment at its core.
- ● *Revolution*: A point is reached in almost all established sciences where the conflicting evidence becomes so overwhelming that the old paradigm has to be abandoned and is replaced by a new one (*paradigm shift*). For example, Newtonian physics was replaced by Einstein's theory of relativity. When this paradigm shift occurs, there is a return to normal science.
- ■ Palermo (1971) and LeFrancois (1983) argue that psychology has already undergone several paradigm shifts. The first paradigm was *structuralism*, represented by Wundt's introspectionism. This was replaced by Watson's behaviourism. Finally, *cognitive psychology* largely replaced *behaviourism*, based on the computer analogy and the concept of information processing. Glassman (1995) disagrees, claiming that there never has been a complete reorganisation of the discipline as has happened in physics.

(Based on Gross, 1996)

Lambie (1991) believes that it is a mistake to equate 'paradigm' with 'approach'. As noted in Table 4.2, whilst theory is an essential part of a paradigm, there is much more involved than this. For example, different theories can coexist within the same overall approach, such as classical and operant conditioning within 'learning theory' (the behaviourist approach), and Freud's and Erikson's theories within the psychodynamic approach.

One of the 'ingredients' that makes a paradigm different from an approach is its *social psychological* dimension. Paradigms refer to assumptions and beliefs held in common by most, if not all, the members of a given scientific community. This issue is discussed further in the following section.

Is it appropriate to study human behaviour using scientific methods?

The social nature of science: the problem of objectivity

'Doing science' is part of human behaviour. When psychologists study what people do, they are engaging in some of the very same behaviours they are trying to understand (such as thinking, perceiving, problem-solving and explaining). This is what is meant by the statement that psychologists are part of their own subject matter, which makes it even more difficult for them to be objective than other scientists.

According to Richards (1996a):

'Whereas in orthodox sciences there is always some external object of enquiry – rocks, electrons, DNA, chemicals – existing essentially unchanging in the non-human world (even if never finally knowable 'as it really is' beyond human conceptions), this is not so for Psychology. 'Doing Psychology' is the human activity of studying human activity; it is human psychology examining itself – and what it produces by way of new theories, ideas and beliefs about itself is also part of our psychology!'.

Knowable 'as it really is' refers to objectivity, and Richards is claiming that it may be impossible for *any* scientist to achieve complete objectivity. One reason for this relates to the social nature of scientific activity. Does this mean that 'the truth' only exists 'by agreement'? Does science tell us not about what things are 'really' like, but only what scientists happen to believe is the truth at any particular time?

EXERCISE 6

Given what was said earlier about the sometimes very intense feelings aroused in individual scientists during the course of their work (see Box 4.5), in what ways do you think science can be described as a social activity? (It might be useful to think about why you do practicals – other than because you have to!)

According to Richardson (1991), whatever the *logical* aspects of scientific method may be (deriving hypotheses from theories, the importance of refutability and so on):

'science is a very *social* business. Yet this exposure of scientific activities to national and international comment and criticism is what distinguishes it from the 'folklore' of informal theories'.

Research must be qualified and quantified to enable others to replicate it, and in this way the procedures, instruments and measures become standardised, so that scientists anywhere in the world can check the truth of reported observations and findings. This implies the need for universally agreed conventions for reporting these observations and findings (Richardson, 1991).

Collins (1994) takes a more extreme view, arguing that the results of experiments are more ambiguous than they are usually taken to be, whilst theory is more flexible than most people imagine:

'This means that science can progress only within communities that can reach consensus about what counts as plausible. Plausibility is a matter of social context so science is a "social construct"' (Collins, 1994).

Kuhn's concept of a paradigm also stresses the role of agreement or consensus among fellow scientists working within a particular discipline. Accordingly, 'truth' has more to do with the popularity and widespread acceptance of a particular framework within the scientific community than with its 'truth value'. The fact that revolutions do occur (paradigm shifts: see Table 4.3, page 103) demonstrates that 'the truth' can and does change.

For example, the change from Newtonian to Einsteinian physics reflected the changing popularity of these two accounts. For Planck, who helped to shape the 'Einsteinian revolution':

'a new scientific theory does not triumph by convincing its opponents and making them see the light, but rather because its opponents eventually die, and a new generation grows up that is familiar with it' (Cited in Kuhn, 1970).

However, the popularity or acceptability of a theory must be at least partly determined by how well it explains and predicts the phenomena in question. In other words, *both* social and 'purely' scientific or rational criteria are relevant.

However, even if there are widely accepted ways of 'doing science', 'good science' does not necessarily mean 'good psychology'. Is it valid to study human behaviour and experience as part of the natural world, or is a different kind of approach needed altogether? After all, it is not just psychologists who observe, experiment and theorise (Heather, 1976).

The psychology experiment as a social situation

To regard empirical research in general, and the experiment in particular, as objective involves two related assumptions. The first is that researchers only influence the *participant's* behaviour (the outcome of the experiment) to the extent that they decide what hypothesis to test, how the variables are to be operationalised, what design to use, and so on. The second assumption is that the only factors influencing the participants' performance are the objectively defined variables manipulated by the experimenter.

EXERCISE 7

Try to formulate some arguments *against* these two assumptions. What do the experimenter and participant bring with them into the experimental situation that is not directly related to the experiment, and how may this (and other factors) influence what goes on in the experimental situation? (See Chapter 5.)

Experimenters are people too: the problem of experimenter bias

According to Rosenthal (1966), what the experimenter is *like* is correlated with what he or she *does*, as well as influencing the participant's perception of, and response to, the experimenter. This is related to *experimenter bias*.

Box 4.6 *Some examples of experimenter bias*

According to Valentine (1992), experimenter bias has been demonstrated in a variety of experiments, including reaction time, psychophysics, non-human learning, verbal conditioning, personality assessment, person perception, learning and ability, as well as in everyday life situations.

What these experiments consistently show is that if one group of experimenters has one hypothesis about what it expects to find and another group has the opposite hypothesis, both groups will obtain results that support their respective hypotheses. The results are *not* due to the mishandling of data by biased experimenters, but the experimenter's bias somehow creates a changed environment, in which participants actually behave differently.

Experimenters who had been informed that rats learning mazes had been specially bred for this ability ('maze-bright'), obtained better learning from their rats than did experimenters who believed that their rats were 'maze-dull' (Rosenthal & Fode, 1963; Rosenthal & Lawson, 1961). In fact, both groups of rats were drawn from the same population and were *randomly* allocated to the 'bright' or 'dull' condition. The crucial point is that the 'bright' rats did actually learn faster. The experimenters' expectations in some way concretely changed the situation, although *how* this happened is far less clear.

In a natural classroom situation, children whose teachers were told that they would show academic 'promise' during the next academic year, showed significantly greater IQ gains than children for whom such predictions were not made (although this group also made substantial improvements). The children were, in fact, *randomly* allocated to the two conditions, but the teachers' expectations actually produced the predicted improvements in the 'academic promise' group, that is, there was a *self-fulfilling* prophecy (Rosenthal & Jacobson, 1968).

(Based on Valentine, 1992, and Weisstein, 1993)

EXERCISE 8

How could you explain the findings from the studies described in Box 4.6? How could experimenter expectations actually bring about the different performances of the two groups of rats and children?

Participants are psychologists too: demand characteristics

Instead of seeing the person being studied as a passive responder to whom things are done ('subject'), Orne (1962) stresses what the person *does*, implying a far more active role. Participants' performance in an experiment could be thought of as a form of problem-solving behaviour. At some level, they see the task as working out the true purpose of the experiment and responding in a way which will support (or not support, in the case of the unhelpful participant) the hypothesis being tested.

In this context, the cues which convey the experimental hypothesis to participants represent important influences on their behaviour, and the sum total of those cues are called *demand characteristics* of the experimental situation. These cues include:

'the rumours or campus scuttlebut [gossip] about the research, the information conveyed during the original situation, the person of the experimenter, and the setting of the laboratory, as well as all explicit and implicit communications during the experiment proper' (Orne, 1962).

This tendency to identify the demand characteristics is related to the tendency to play the role of a 'good' (or 'bad') experimental participant.

Box 4.7   *The lengths that some people will go to to please the experimenter*

Orne points out that if people are asked to do five push-ups as a favour, they will ask 'Why?', but if the request comes from an experimenter, they will ask 'Where?' Similarly, he reports an experiment in which people were asked to add sheets of random numbers, then tear them up into at least 32 pieces. Five-and-a-half hours later, they were still at it and the experimenter had to stop them!

This demonstrates very clearly the strong tendency to want to please the experimenter, and not to 'upset the experiment'. It is mainly in this sense that Orne sees the experiment as a social situation, in which the people involved play different but complementary roles. In order for this interaction to proceed fairly smoothly, each must have some idea of what the other expects of him or her.

The expectations referred to in Box 4.7 are part of the culturally shared understandings of what science in general, and psychology in particular, involves and without which the experiment could not 'happen' (Moghaddam *et al.*, 1993). So not only is the experiment a social situation, but science itself is a *culture-related phenomenon*. This represents another respect in which science cannot claim complete objectivity.

The problem of representativeness

Traditional, mainstream experimental psychology adopts a *nomothetic* ('law-like') approach. This involves generalisation from limited samples of participants to 'people in general', as part of the attempt to establish general 'laws' or principles of behaviour (see Figure 4.5, page 98).

EXERCISE 9

Figure 4.6 captures a fairly typical scene as far as participant characteristics in mainstream psychological research are concerned.

In this photograph of one of Asch's famous conformity experiments, what are the most apparent characteristics of the experimental participants, and how are they similar to/different from those of Asch (who is pictured furthest right)?

Despite the fact that Asch's experiments were carried out in the early 1950s, very little has changed as far as participant samples are concerned. In American psychology, at least, the typical participant is a psychology undergraduate, who is obliged to take part in a certain number of studies as a course requirement and who receives 'course credit' for so doing (Krupat & Garonzik, 1994).

Mainstream British and American psychology has implicitly equated 'human being' with 'member of Western culture'. Despite the fact that the vast majority of research participants are members of Western societies, the resulting findings and theories have been applied to 'human beings', as if culture made no difference. This Anglocentric or Eurocentric bias (a form of *ethnocentrism*) is matched by the androcentric or masculinist bias (a form of *sexism*), according to which the behaviours and experiences of men are taken as the standard against which women are judged (see Chapter 5).

In both cases, whilst the bias remains implicit and goes unrecognised (and is reinforced by psychology's claim to be objective and value-free), research findings are taken as providing us with an objective, scientifically valid, account of what 'women/people in general are like'. Once we realise that scientists, like all human beings, have prejudices, biases and values, their research and theory begin to look less objective, reliable and valid than they did before (see Chapter 5).

The problem of artificiality

Criticisms of traditional empirical methods (especially the laboratory experiment) have focused on their *artificiality*, including the often unusual and bizarre tasks that people are asked to perform in the name of science (see Box 4.7). Yet we cannot be sure that the way people behave in the laboratory is an accurate indication of how they are likely to behave outside it (Heather, 1976).

What makes the laboratory experiment such an unnatural and artificial situation is the fact that it is almost totally structured by one 'participant' – the experimenter. This relates to *power differences* between experimenters and their 'subjects', which is as much an *ethical* as a practical issue and is discussed further in Chapter 6.

Traditionally, participants have been referred to as 'subjects', implying something less than a person, a dehumanised and depersonalised 'object'. According to Heather (1976), it is a small step from reducing the person to a mere thing or object (or experimental 'subject'), to seeing people as machines or machine-like ('mechanism' = 'machine-ism' = mechanistic view of people). This way of thinking about people is reflected in the popular definition of psychology as the study of 'what makes people tick' (see Chapter 1 and pages 87–88).

The problem of internal versus external validity

If the experimental setting (and task) is seen as similar or relevant enough to everyday situations to allow us to generalise the results, we say that the study has high *external* or *ecological validity*. But what about *internal validity*? Modelling itself on natural science, psychology attempts to overcome the problem of the complexity of human behaviour by using *experimental control*. This involves isolating an independent variable (IV) and ensuring that extraneous variables (variables other than the IV likely to affect the dependent variable) do not affect the outcome. But this begs the crucial question: *how do we know when all the relevant extraneous variables have been controlled?*

Box 4.8 *Some difficulties with the notion of experimental control*

- Whilst it is relatively easy to control the more obvious *situational variables*, this is more difficult with *participant variables* (such as age, gender and culture), either for practical reasons (such as the availability of these groups), or because it is not always obvious exactly what the relevant variables are. Ultimately, it is down to the experimenter's judgement and intuition: what he or she believes is important (and possible) to control (Deese, 1972).

- If judgement and intuition are involved, then control and objectivity are matters of degree, whether it is in psychology or physics (see Table 4.1, page 99).

- It is the *variability/heterogeneity* of human beings that makes them so much more difficult to study than, say, chemicals. Chemists don't usually have to worry about how two samples of a particular chemical might be different from each other, but psychologists definitely do have to allow for individual differences between participants.

- We cannot just assume that the IV (or 'stimulus' or 'input') is identical for every participant, and can be defined in some objective way, independently of the participant, exerting a standard effect on everyone. The attempt to define IVs (and DVs) in this way can be regarded as a form of reductionism (see Chapter 2).

- Complete control would mean that the IV alone was responsible for the DV, so that experimenter bias and the effect of demand characteristics were irrelevant. But even if complete control were possible (even if we could guarantee the *internal validity* of the experiment), a fundamental dilemma would remain. The greater the degree of control over the experimental situation, the more different it becomes from real-life situations (the more artificial it gets and the lower its *external validity*).

As Box 4.8 indicates, in order to discover the relationships between variables (necessary for understanding human behaviour in natural, real-life situations), psychologists must 'bring' the behaviour into a specially created environment (the laboratory), where the relevant variables can be controlled in a way that is impossible in naturally-occurring settings. However, in doing so, psychologists have constructed an artificial environment and the resulting behaviour is similarly artificial. It is no longer the behaviour they were trying to understand!

Conclusions

Psychology as a separate field of study grew out of several other disciplines, both scientific (such as physiology), and non-scientific (in particular philosophy). For much of its life as an independent discipline, and through what some call revolutions and paradigm shifts, it has taken the natural sciences as its model (scientism). This chapter has highlighted some of the major implications of adopting methods of investigating the natural world and applying them to the study of human behaviour and experience. In doing this, the chapter has also examined what are fast becoming out-dated and inaccurate views about the nature of science. Ultimately, whatever a particular science may claim to have discovered about the phenomena it studies, scientific activity remains just one more aspect of human behaviour.

Summary

- **Philosophical dualism** enabled scientists to describe the world **objectively**, which became the ideal of science. Its extension by Comte to the study of human behaviour and social institutions is called **positivism**. Descartes extended **mechanism** to the human body, but the mind remained accessible only through **introspection**.

- **Empirism** emphasises the importance of sensory experience, as opposed to **nativism's** claim that knowledge is innate. 'Empirical' implies that the essence of science is collecting data/'facts' through experiments and observations. **Empiricism** influenced psychology through its influence on physiology, physics and chemistry.

- Wundt is generally regarded as the founder of the new science of experimental psychology, establishing its first laboratory in 1879. He used **introspection** to study conscious experience, analysing it into its basic elements (**sensations** and **feelings**). This is called **structuralism**.

- James is the other pioneer of scientific psychology. He influenced several important research areas, and helped make Freud's ideas popular in America. His views influenced **functionalism** which, in turn, stimulated interest in individual differences.

- Watson's criticisms of introspection culminated in his 1913 'behaviourist manifesto'. He argued that for psychology to be objective, it must study behaviour rather than mental life, its goals should be the prediction and control of **behaviour**, and there are only **quantitative** differences between human and non-human behaviour. The conditioned reflex could become the basis of a full-scale human psychology.

- Instead of the mind being influenced by experience (as Locke believed), Watson saw **behaviour** as shaped by the environment. Empirism provided for psychology both a **methodology** and a **theory** (including analysis into elements and **associationism**). Consciousness and subjective experience had no place in the behaviourist world and people were studied as 'natural phenomena'.

- Dissatisfaction with behaviourism culminated in the 1956 'cognitive revolution'. At the centre of this new **information-processing approach** lay the **computer analogy**.

- Despite this major change, **mainstream** psychology (the 'old paradigm') has survived. **Scientism** maintains that all aspects of human behaviour can and should be studied using the methods of natural science, and involves 'context-stripping' and the **value-free**, objective use of laboratory experiments in particular. People are seen as passive and mechanical information-processing devices and treated as interchangeable 'subjects'.

- A science must possess a definable **subject matter**, involve **theory construction** and **hypothesis testing**, and use **empirical methods** for data collection. However, these characteristics fail to describe the **scientific process** or **scientific method**, about which there are several common misconceptions. Whilst the classical view of science is built around the **inductive method**, Popper's revised view stresses the **hypothetico-deductive method**. The two methods are complementary.

- Different theoretical **approaches** can be seen as self-contained disciplines, making psychology **pre-paradigmatic** and so still in a stage of **pre-science**. According to Kuhn, only when a discipline possesses a paradigm has it reached the stage of **normal science**, after which **paradigm shifts** result in **revolution** (and a return to normal science). However, 'paradigm' and 'approach' are different, with the former involving a **social psychological** dimension.

- Even where there are external objects of scientific enquiry (as in chemistry), complete objectivity may be impossible. Whatever the **logical** aspects of scientific method may be, science is a very **social** activity. Consensus among colleagues is paramount, as shown by the fact that revolutions involve re-defining 'the truth'.

- **Experimenter bias** and **demand characteristics** make psychological research (especially experiments) even less objective than natural sciences. Environmental changes are somehow produced by experimenters' expectations, and demand characteristics influence participants' behaviours by helping to convey the experimental hypothesis. Their performance is a form of problem-solving behaviour and reflects their playing the roles of 'good' (or 'bad') experimental participants. The experiment is a social situation and science itself is **culture-related**.

- The **artificiality** of laboratory experiments is largely due to their being totally structured by experimenters. Also, the higher an experiment's **internal validity**, the lower its **external validity** becomes. Whilst certain **situational variables** can be controlled quite easily, this is more difficult with **participant variables**.

BIAS IN PSYCHOLOGICAL THEORY AND RESEARCH

Introduction and overview

As was seen in Chapter 4, mainstream academic psychology, modelling itself on classical, orthodox, natural science (such as physics and chemistry), claims to be *objective*, *unbiased*, and *value-free* (collectively referred to as the *positivist* view of science, or *positivism*). As applied to the study of humans, this implies that it is possible to study people as they 'really are', without the psychologist's characteristics influencing the outcome of the investigation in any way.

This chapter shows that a view of psychology as unbiased and value-free is mistaken. It discusses two major forms of bias (namely, *sexism* and *ethnocentrism*, relating to gender and culture respectively) which permeate much psychological theory and research.

Much of this chapter's content is relevant to the topic of prejudice and discrimination, which can be understood as characteristics of *individuals* or of *social groups*, *institutions* and even *whole societies*. With bias in psychological theory and research, it is sometimes individual psychologists, and sometimes 'psychology as a whole' that are being accused.

Gender bias: feminist psychology, sexism and androcentrism

Not surprisingly, most of the criticism of mainstream psychology regarding its gender bias has come from *feminist psychology*, which Wilkinson (1997) defines as:

'... psychological theory and practice which is explicitly informed by the political goals of the feminist movement ...'.

Whilst feminism can take a variety of forms, two common themes are the valuation of women as worthy of study in their own right (not just in comparison with men), and recognition of the need for social change on behalf of women.

Feminist psychology is openly political (Unger & Crawford, 1992) and sets out to challenge the discipline of psychology for its inadequate and damaging theories about women, and for its failure to see power relations as central to social life. More specifically, it insists on exposing and challenging the operation of male power in psychology:

> '... psychology's theories often exclude women, or distort our experience by assimilating it to male norms or man-made stereotypes, or by regarding "women" as a unitary category, to be understood only in comparison with the unitary category "men" ... Similarly, psychology [screens out] ... the existence and operation of social and structural inequalities between and within social groups ... ' (Wilkinson, 1991).

Psychology obscures the social and structural operation of male power by concentrating its analysis on people as individuals (*individualism*). Responsibility (and pathology) are located within the individual, to the total neglect of social and political oppression. By ignoring or minimising the *social context*, psychology obscures the mechanisms of oppression. For example, the unhappiness of some women after childbirth is treated as a problem in individual functioning (with possible hormonal causes), thus distracting attention away from the difficult material situation in which many new mothers find themselves (Wilkinson, 1997).

Box 5.1 *Some major feminist criticisms of psychology*

- Much psychological research is conducted on all-male samples, but then either fails to make this clear or reports the findings as if they applied equally to women and men.
- Some of the most influential theories within psychology as a whole are based on studies of males only, but are meant to apply equally to women and men.
- If women's behaviour differs from men's, the former is often judged to be pathological, abnormal or deficient in some way

(*sexism*), since the behaviour of men is, implicitly or explicitly, taken as the 'standard' or norm against which women's behaviour is compared (*androcentrism*, male-centredness, or the *masculinist bias*).

- Psychological explanations of behaviour tend to emphasise biological (and other internal) causes (*individualism*), as opposed to social (and other external) causes. This gives (and reinforces) the impression that psychological sex differences are inevitable and unchangeable. This reinforces widely held stereotypes about men and women, contributing to the oppression of women (another form of *sexism*).
- Heterosexuality (both male and female) is taken, implicitly or explicitly, as the norm, so that homosexuality is seen as abnormal (*heterosexism*).

EXERCISE 1

Try to think of (at least) one example for each of the five major criticisms of psychological theory and research made in Box 5.1. Regarding the fourth point, how does this relate to attribution theory? (see Gross & McIlveen, 1998).

The feminist critique of science

In many ways, a more fundamental criticism of psychology than those listed in Box 5.1 is feminists' belief that scientific enquiry itself (whether this be within psychology or not) is biased.

Psychology's claims to be a science are based on its methods (especially the experiment) and the belief that it is a value-free discipline (see Chapter 4). However, as far as the latter is concerned, can scientific enquiry be neutral, wholly independent of the value system of the human scientists involved? According to Prince & Hartnett (1993):

'Decisions about what is, and what is not, to be measured, how this is done, and most importantly, what constitutes legitimate research are made by individual scientists within a socio-political context, and thus science is ideological ...'.

As far as scientific method is concerned, many feminist psychologists argue that it is itself gender-biased. For example, Nicolson (1995) identifies two major problems associated with adherence to the 'objective' investigation of behaviour for the way knowledge claims are made about women and gender differences.

First, the experimental environment takes the individual 'subject's *behaviour*' as distinct from the 'subject' herself as the unit of study. Therefore, it becomes deliberately blind to the behaviour's *meaning*, including the social, personal and cultural contexts in which it is enacted. As a result, claims about gender differences in competence and behaviour are attributed to intrinsic (either the product of 'gender role socialisation' or biology) as opposed to contextual qualities. This is another reference to *individualism* (see page 118).

Second, experimental psychology, far from being context-free, takes place in a very specific context which typically disadvantages women (Eagly, 1987). In an experiment, a woman becomes anonymous, stripped of her social roles and accompanying power and knowledge she might have achieved in the outside world. She is placed in this 'strange', environment, and expected to respond to the needs of (almost inevitably) a male experimenter who is in charge of the situation, with all the social meaning ascribed to gender power relations.

The belief that it is possible to study people 'as they really are', removed from their usual socio-cultural context (in a 'de-contextualised' way), is completely invalid:

'Psychology relies for its data on the practices of socialised and culture-bound individuals, so that to explore 'natural' or 'culture-free' behaviour (namely that behaviour unfettered by cultural, social structures and power relations) is by definition impossible ...' (Nicolson, 1995).

Feminist psychologists offer a critical challenge to psychological knowledge on gender issues by drawing on other disciplines, such as sociology. According to Giddens (1979), for example:

'There is no static knowledge about people to be 'discovered' or 'proved' through reductionist experimentation, and thus the researcher takes account of context, meaning and change over time'.

EXERCISE 2

Do you agree with Nicolson's claim that all human behaviour is 'culture-bound? What about 'instinctive' behaviours, such as eating, drinking and sex: does culture play a part here too? If so, in what ways? (These questions are equally relevant to the section on culture bias.)

Some practical consequences of gender bias

For Prince & Hartnett (1993), scientific psychology has *reified* concepts such as personality and intelligence (treating abstract or metaphorical terms as if they were 'things' or entities):

'... and the scientific psychology which 'objectively' and 'rationally' produced means of measuring these reifications has been responsible for physical assaults on women such as forced abortions and sterilisations'.

Between 1924 and 1972, more than 7500 women in the state of Virginia alone were forcibly sterilised, in particular, 'unwed mothers, prisoners, the feeble-minded, children with discipline problems'. The criterion used in all cases was mental age as measured by the Stanford–Binet intelligence test (Gould, 1981).

Having convinced society that intelligence 'exists' in some objective way, and having produced a means of measuring it, psychologists could then promote and justify discrimination against particular social groups. Another example of the use of intelligence tests to justify blatant discrimination (although not specifically against women) involved the army alpha and beta tests (see Chapter 3), which influenced the passing of the 1924 Immigration Restriction Act in the USA.

Box 5.2 *Psychology's influence on immigration policy in the USA*

Debates in Congress leading to passage of the Immigration Restriction Act of 1924 continually made reference to data from the army alpha and beta tests. Eugenicists (those who advocate 'selective breeding' in humans in order to 'improve' genetic stock) lobbied for immigration limits and for imposing harsh quotas against nations of inferior stock. In short, Southern and Eastern Europeans, who scored lowest on the army tests, should be kept out. The eugenicists battled and won one of the greatest victories of scientific racism in American history. 'America must be kept American', proclaimed President Coolidge as he signed the bill.

Throughout the 1930s, Jewish refugees, anticipating the Holocaust, sought to emigrate, but were refused admission. Estimates suggest that the quotas barred up to six million Southern, Central and Eastern Europeans between 1924 and 1939.

'We know what happened to many who wished to leave, but had nowhere to go. The paths to destruction are often indirect, but ideas can be agents as sure as guns and bombs' (Gould, 1981).

(From Gould, 1981)

In the 1993 preface to *In a Different Voice* (1982), Gilligan says that at the core of her work on moral development in women and girls (see below) was the realisation that within psychology, and in society at large, 'values were taken as facts'. She continues:

' ... in the aftermath of the Holocaust ... it is not tenable for psychologists or social scientists to adopt a position of ethical neutrality or cultural relativism ... Such a hands-off stance in the face of atrocity amounts to a kind of complicity'.

Whilst the example she gives is clearly extreme, it helps to illustrate the argument that not only do psychologists (and other scientists) have a responsibility to make their values explicit about important social and political issues, but failure to do so may (unwittingly) contribute to prejudice, discrimination and oppression. These considerations are as relevant to a discussion of the ethics of psychological research as they are to gender (and culture) bias, and are discussed in more detail in Chapter 6.

The masculinist bias and sexism: a closer look

Box 5.1 identified the masculinist bias (*androcentrism*) and sexism as two major criticisms of mainstream psychology made by feminist psychologists. Whilst each of these can take different forms, emphasis here will be given to (a) the argument that men are taken as some sort of standard or norm, against which women are compared and judged, and (b) gender bias in psychological research.

The male norm as the standard

According to Tavris (1993):

'In any domain of life in which men set the standard of normalcy, women will be considered abnormal, and society will debate woman's 'place' and her 'nature'. Many women experience tremendous conflict in trying to decide whether to be 'like' men or 'opposite' from them, and this conflict is itself evidence of the implicit male standard against which they are measuring themselves. This is why it is normal for women to feel abnormal'.

She gives two examples of why it is normal for women to feel abnormal. First, in 1985, the American Psychiatric Association proposed two new categories of mental disorder for inclusion in the revised (third) edition of the *Diagnostic and Statistical Manual of Mental Disorders* (DSM-III-R). One was *masochistic personality*. In DSM-II this was described as one of the psychosexual disorders in which sexual gratification requires being hurt or humiliated. The proposal was to extend the term so that it became a more pervasive personality disorder, in which one seeks failure at work, at home, and in relationships, rejects opportunities for pleasure, puts others first, thereby sacrificing one's own needs, plays the martyr, and so on.

Whilst not intended to apply to women exclusively, these characteristics are associated predominantly with the female role. Indeed, according to Caplan (1991), it represented a way of calling psychopathological the behaviour of women who conform to social norms for a 'feminine woman' (the 'good wife syndrome').

In short, such a diagnostic label was biased against women and perpetuated the myth of women's masochism. The label was eventually changed to *self-defeating personality disorder* and was put in the appendix of DSM-III-R.

EXERCISE 3

If you were proposing a parallel diagnosis for men who conform to social norms for a 'masculine man', what characteristics would this have to include, and what would you call it? Could you justify extending *sadism* to conformist men?

Tavris's second example of why it is normal for women to feel abnormal concerns causal attributions made about men's and women's behaviours. When men have problems, such as drug abuse, and behave in socially unacceptable ways, as in rape and other forms of violence, the causes are looked for in their upbringings. Women's problems, however, are seen as the result of their psyches or hormones. This is another form of *individualism*, with the further implication that it could have been different for men (they are the victims of their childhood, for example), but not for women ('that's what women are like').

The 'mismeasure of woman'

According to Tavris, the view that man is the norm and woman is the opposite, lesser or deficient (the problem) constitutes one of three currently competing views regarding the 'mismeasure of woman' (meant to parallel Gould's, 1981, *The Mismeasure of Man*, a renowned critique of intelligence testing: see Chapter 3). It is the view that underpins so much psychological research designed to discover why women aren't 'as something' (moral, intelligent, rational) as men. It also underlies the enormous self-help industry, whereby women consume millions of books and magazines advising them how to become more beautiful, independent and so on. Men, being normal, feel no need to 'fix' themselves in corresponding ways (Tavris, 1993).

Box 5.3 *A demonstration of the 'mismeasure of woman'*

Wilson (1994) states that the reason 95 per cent of bank managers, company directors, judges and university professors in Britain are men is that men are 'more competitive' and because 'dominance is a personality characteristic determined by male hormones'.

He also argues that women in academic jobs are less productive than men: 'objectively speaking, women may already be over-promoted'. Women who *do* achieve promotion to top management positions 'may have brains that are masculinised'.

The research cited by Wilson to support these claims comes partly from the psychometric testing industries (see Chapter 3) which provide 'scientific' evidence of women's inadequacies, such as (compared with men) their lack of mathematical and spatial abilities. Even if women are considered to have the abilities to perform well in professional jobs, they have personality defects (in particular, low self-esteem and lack of assertiveness) which impede performance. According to Wilson (1994):

'These differences [in mental abilities, motivation, personality and values] are deep-rooted, based in biology, and not easily dismantled by social engineering. Because of them we are unlikely to see the day when the occupational profiles of men and women are the same …'.

(From Wilson, 1994, and Wilkinson, 1997)

EXERCISE 4

In Box 5.3, try to identify examples of *individualism*. Can you formulate some arguments *against* Wilson's claims?

Sexism in research

The American Psychological Association's Board of Social and Ethical Responsibility set up a Committee on Nonsexist Research, which reported its findings as *Guidelines for Avoiding Sexism in Psychological Research* (Denmark *et al.*, 1988). This maintains that gender bias is found at all stages of the research process: (i) question formulation (ii) research methods and design (iii) data analysis and interpretation, and (iv) conclusion formulation. The principles set out in the *Guidelines* are meant to apply to other forms of bias too: race, ethnicity, disability, sexual orientation and socio-economic status.

Box 5.4 *Examples of gender bias at each stage of the research process*

- **Question formulation:** It is assumed that topics relevant to white males are more important and 'basic' (e.g. the effects of TV violence on aggression in boys), whilst those relevant to white females, or ethnic minority females or males, are more marginal, specialised, or applied (e.g. the psychological correlates of pregnancy or the menopause).

- **Research methods and design:** Surprisingly often, the sex and race of the participants, researchers, and any confederates who may be involved, are not specified. As a consequence, potential interactions between these variables are not accounted for. For example, men tend to display more helping behaviour than women in studies involving a young, female confederate 'victim'. This could be a function of either the sex of the confederate or an interaction between the confederate and the participant, rather than sex differences between the participants (which is the conclusion usually drawn).

- **Data analysis and interpretation:** Significant *sex differences* may be reported in very misleading ways, because the wrong sorts of comparisons are made. For example:

    'The spatial ability scores of women in our sample is significantly lower than those of men, at the 0.01 level'. You might conclude from this that women cannot or should not become architects or engineers. However, 'Successful architects score above 32 on our spatial ability test ... engineers score above 31 ... 12 per cent of women and 16 per cent of men in our sample score above 31; 11 per cent of women and 15 per cent of men score above 32'. What conclusions would you draw now? (Denmark *et al.*, 1988)

- **Conclusion formulation:** Results based on one sex only are then applied to both. This can be seen in some of the major theories within developmental psychology, notably Erikson's (1950) psychosocial theory of development, Levinson *et al.*'s (1978) *Seasons of a Man's Life*, and Kohlberg's (1969) theory of moral development. These are discussed further below.

(Based on Denmark *et al.*, 1988)

Sexism in theory

Gilligan (1982) gives Erikson's theory of lifespan development (based on the study of males only) as one example of a sexist theory, which portrays women as 'deviants'. In one version of his theory, Erikson (1950) describes a series of eight *universal* stages, so that, for both sexes, in all cultures, the conflict between *identity* and *role confusion* (adolescence) precedes that between *intimacy* and *isolation* (young adulthood). In another version, he acknowledges that the sequence is *different* for the female, who postpones her identity as she prepares to attract the man whose name she will adopt, and by whose status she will be defined (Erikson, 1968). For women, intimacy seems to go along with identity: they come to know themselves through their relationships with others (Gilligan, 1982).

Despite his observation of sex differences, Erikson's *epigenetic chart* of the life-cycle remains unchanged. As Gilligan points out:

'identity continues to precede intimacy as male experience continues to define his [Erikson's] life-cycle concept'.

Similarly, Kohlberg's (1969) six-stage theory of moral development was based on a 20-year longitudinal study of 84 boys, but he claims that these stages are universal. Females rarely attain a level of moral reasoning above stage three ('Good boy–nice girl' orientation), which is supposed to be achieved by most adolescents and adults. This leaves females looking decidedly morally deficient.

Like other feminist psychologists, Gilligan argues that psychology speaks with a 'male voice', describing the world from a male perspective and confusing this with absolute truth. The task of feminist psychology is to listen to women and girls who speak in a 'different voice' (Gilligan, 1982; Brown & Gilligan, 1992). Gilligan's work with females has led her to argue that men and women have qualitatively different conceptions of morality, with moral dilemmas being 'solved' in terms of care, responsibility and relationships. Men are more likely to stress rights and rules.

EXERCISE 5

In what ways is Freud's psychoanalytic theory (especially the psychosexual stages of development) sexist (or what Grosz, 1987, calls 'phallocentric')? Repeat this exercise for Levinson *et al.*'s theory of adult development, and any other theory you are familiar with.

Culture bias

In discussing gender bias, several references have been made to cultural bias. Denmark *et al.*'s (1988) report on sexism is meant to apply equally to all other major forms of bias, including cultural (see Box 5.4). Ironically, many feminist critics of Gilligan's ideas have argued that women are not a cohesive group who speak in a single voice, a view which imposes a false sameness upon the diversity of women's voices across differences of age, ethnicity, (dis)ability, class and other social divisions (Wilkinson, 1997).

EXERCISE 6

Before reading on, ask yourself what is meant by the term 'culture'. How is it related to 'race', 'ethnicity' and 'sub-cultures'?

Cross-cultural psychology and ethnocentrism

According to Smith & Bond (1993), cross-cultural psychology studies variability in behaviour among the various societies and cultural groups around the world. For Jahoda (1978), its additional goal is to identify what is similar across different cultures, and thus likely to be our common human heritage (the universals of human behaviour).

Cross-cultural psychology is important because it helps to correct *ethnocentrism*, the strong human tendency to use our own ethnic or cultural groups' norms and values to define what is 'natural' and 'correct' for everyone ('reality': Triandis, 1990).

Historically, psychology has been dominated by white, middle class males in the USA. Over the last century, they have enjoyed a monopoly as both the researchers and the 'subjects' of the discipline (Moghaddam & Studer, 1997). They constitute the core of psychology's First World (Moghaddam, 1987).

Box 5.5 *Psychology's First, Second and Third Worlds*

- The USA, the *First World* of psychology, dominates the international arena and monopolises the manufacture of psychological knowledge, which it exports to other countries around the globe, through control over books and journals, test manufacture and distribution, training centres and so on.
- The *Second World* countries comprise Western European nations and Russia. They have far less influence in shaping psychology around the world, although, ironically, it is in these countries that modern psychology has its philosophical roots (see Chapter 4). Just as the countries of the Second World find themselves overpowered by US pop culture, they also find themselves overwhelmed by US-manufactured psychological knowledge.
- *Third World* countries are mostly importers of psychological knowledge, first from the USA but also from the Second World countries with which they historically had colonial ties (such as Pakistan and England). India is the most important Third World 'producer' of psychological knowledge, but even there most research follows the lines established by the US and, to a lesser extent, Western Europe.

(From Moghaddam & Studer, 1997)

According to Moghaddam *et al.* (1993), American researchers and participants:

'have shared a lifestyle and value system that differs not only from that of most other people in North America, such as ethnic minorities and women, but also the vast majority of people in the rest of the world'.

Yet the findings from this research, and the theories based upon it, have been applied to *people in general*, as if culture makes no difference. An implicit equation is made between 'human being' and 'human being from Western culture' (the *Anglocentric* or *Eurocentric bias*).

When members of other cultural groups have been studied, it has usually been to compare them with Western samples, using the behaviour and experience of the latter as the 'standard'. As with androcentrism, it is the failure to acknowledge this bias which creates the misleading and false impression that what is being said about behaviour can be generalised without qualification.

Cross-cultural psychologists do *not* equate 'human being' with 'member of Western culture', because for them, cultural background is the crucial *independent variable*. In view of the domination of First World psychology, this distinction becomes crucial. At the same time, the search for universal principles of human behaviour is quite valid (and is consistent with the 'classical' view of science: see Chapter 4).

What is culture?

Herskovits (1955) defines culture as 'the human-made part of the environment'. For Triandis (1994):

> **'Culture is to society what memory is to individuals. In other words, culture includes the traditions that tell 'what has worked' in the past. It also encompasses the way people have learned to look at their environment and themselves, and their unstated assumptions about the way the world is and the way people should act'.**

The 'human-made' part of the environment can be broken down into *objective* aspects (such as tools, roads, radio stations) and *subjective* aspects (such as categorisations, associations, norms, roles, values). This allows us to examine how subjective culture influences behaviour (Triandis, 1994). Whilst culture is made by humans, it also helps to 'make' them: humans have an interactive relationship with culture (Moghaddam *et al.*, 1993).

Much cross-cultural research is actually based on 'national cultures', often comprising a number of sub-cultures, which may be demarcated by religion (as in Northern Ireland), language

(Belgium), or race (Malaysia and Singapore). However, such research often fails to provide any more details about the participants than the name of the country (national culture) in which the study was done. When this happens, we pay two 'penalties'.

First, when we compare national cultures, we can lose track of the enormous diversity found within many of the major nations of the world, and differences found *between* any two countries might well also be found between carefully selected subcultures *within* those countries. Second, there is the danger of implying that national cultures are unitary systems, free of conflict, confusion and dissent. This is rarely the case (Smith & Bond, 1993).

How do cultures differ?

Definitions of culture such as those above stress what *different cultures* have in common. To evaluate research findings and theory that are culturally biased, it is even more important to consider the ways in which *cultures are different* from each other. Triandis (1990) identifies several *cultural syndromes*, which he defines as:

'a pattern of values, attitudes, beliefs, norms and behaviours that can be used to contrast a group of cultures to another group of cultures'.

Box 5.6   *Three major cultural syndromes used to contrast different cultures*

Three major cultural syndromes are *cultural complexity, individualism–collectivism*, and *tight vs. loose cultures*.

- **Cultural complexity** refers to how much attention people must pay to *time*. This is related to the number and diversity of the roles that members of the culture typically play. More industrialised and technologically advanced cultures, such as Japan, Sweden and the USA are more complex in this way. (The *concept* of time also differs between cultures.)
- **Individualism–collectivism** refers to whether one's identity is defined by personal choices and achievements (the autonomous individual: *individualism*) or by characteristics of the collective

---

group to which one is more or less permanently attached, such as the family, tribal or religious group, or country (*collectivism*). Whilst people in every culture display both, the relative emphasis in the West is towards individualism and in the East towards collectivism. Broadly, *capitalist* politico-economic systems are associated with individualism, whilst *socialist* societies are associated with collectivism.

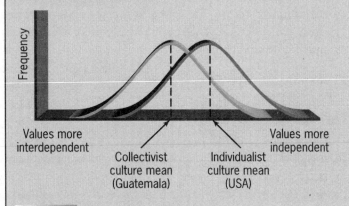

Values more interdependent

Collectivist culture mean (Guatemala)

Individualist culture mean (USA)

Values more independent

Figure 5.1 *Hypothetical distributions of interdependent/independent value scores in a collectivist and an individualist national culture (From Smith & Bond, 1993)*

● **Tight** cultures expect their members to behave according to clearly defined norms, and there is very little tolerance of deviation from those norms (such as the criteria of normality/ abnormality). Japan is a good example of a tight culture, and Thailand an example of a loose culture.
(Based on Smith & Bond, 1993, and Triandis, 1990, 1994)

The emic–etic distinction

Research has to begin somewhere and, inevitably, this usually involves an instrument or observational technique rooted in the researcher's own culture (Berry, 1969). These can be used for studying *both* cross-cultural differences *and* universal aspects of human behaviour (or the 'psychic unity of mankind').

EXERCISE 7

Try to identify some behaviours (both normal and abnormal) which can be considered to have both universal (i.e. common to all cultures) *and* culture-specific features.

The distinction between culture-specific and universal behaviour is related to what cross-cultural psychologists call the *emic–etic distinction*, first made by Pike (1954) to refer to two different approaches to the study of behaviour. The *etic* looks at behaviour from outside a particular cultural system, the *emic* from the inside. This derives from the distinction made in linguistics between phon*etics* (the study of universal sounds, independently of their meaning) and phon*emics* (the study of universal sounds as they contribute to meaning).

'Etics' refers to culturally general concepts, which are easier to understand (because they are common to all cultures), whilst 'emics' refers to culturally specific concepts, which include all the ways that particular cultures deal with etics. It is the emics of another culture that are often so difficult to understand (Brislin, 1993).

The research tools that the 'visiting' psychologist brings from 'home' are an emic for the home culture, but when they are assumed to be valid in the 'alien' culture and are used to compare them, they are said to be an *imposed etic* (Berry, 1969). Many attempts to replicate American studies in other parts of the world involve an imposed etic: they all assume that the situation being studied has the same meaning for members of the alien culture as it does for members of the researcher's own culture (Smith & Bond, 1993).

The danger of imposed etics is that they are likely to involve imposition of the researcher's own cultural biases and theoretical framework which simply may not 'fit' the phenomena being studied, resulting in their distortion. A related danger is ethnocentrism (see above).

> **Box 5.7** *Intelligence as an imposed etic*
>
> Brislin (1993) gives the example of the concept of intelligence. The etic is 'solving problems, the exact form of which hasn't been seen before', a definition which at least recognises that what constitutes a 'problem' differs between cultures. However, is the emic of 'mental quickness' (as measured by IQ tests, for example) universally valid? Among the Baganda people of Uganda, for example, intelligence is associated with slow, careful, deliberate thought (Wober, 1974). Nor is quick thinking necessarily a valid emic for all schoolchildren within a culturally diverse country like the USA (Brislin, 1993).

Psychologists need to adapt their methods, so that they are studying the same processes in different cultures (Moghaddam *et al.*, 1993). But how do we know that we are studying the same processes? What does 'same' mean in this context? For Brislin (1993), this is the problem of *equivalence*. For a detailed discussion of different kinds of equivalence, see Gross (1995).

Advantages of cross-cultural research

It may now seem obvious (almost 'common sense') to state that psychological theories must be based on the study of people's behaviours from all parts of the world. However, it is important to give specific reasons and examples in support of this argument.

> **Box 5.8** *Major advantages of cross-cultural research*
>
> ● **Highlighting implicit assumptions:** Cross-cultural research allows investigators to examine the influence of their own beliefs and assumptions, revealing how human behaviour cannot be separated from its cultural context.
> ● **Separating behaviour from context:** Being able to stand back from their own cultural experiences allows researchers to appreciate the impact of situational factors on behaviour. They are thus less likely to make the *fundamental attribution error*, or to use a 'deficit model' to explain the performances of minority group members.

- **Extending the range of variables:** Cross-cultural research expands the range of variables and concepts that can be explored. For example, people in individualist and collectivist cultures tend to explain behaviour in different ways, with the latter less likely to make *dispositional attributions*.
- **Separating variables:** Cross-cultural research allows the separation of the effects of variables that may be confounded within a particular culture. For example, studying the effects of television on school achievement is very difficult using just British or American samples, since the vast majority of these families own (at least) one TV set!
- **Testing theories:** Only by conducting cross-cultural research can Western psychologists be sure whether their theories and research findings are relevant outside of their own cultural contexts. For example, Thibaut & Kelley's (1959) exchange theory of relationships, and Sherif *et al.*'s (1961) 'Robber's Cave' field experiment on intergroup conflict have all failed the replication test outside of North American settings.

(Based on Rogoff & Morelli, 1989; Brislin, 1993; Moghaddam *et al.*, 1993, and Smith & Bond, 1993)

Conclusions

This chapter has considered many different examples of how mainstream psychology is biased and, therefore, much less objective and value-free than is required by the positivist view of science it has traditionally modelled itself on. Whilst gender and culture bias are often discussed separately, this chapter has shown that they are actually quite closely related. Despite its shortcomings, Moghaddam & Studer (1997) believe that cross-cultural psychology is one of the avenues through which minorities have begun to have their voices heard in psychology and that:

' there has been a demand that psychology make good its claim to being the science of *humankind* by including women and non-whites as research participants ...'.

Summary

- A **positivist** study of people implies an objective, value-free psychology, in which the psychologist's characteristics have no influence on the investigation's outcome. However, **sexism** and **ethnocentrism** pervade much psychological theory and research.

- **Feminist psychologists** challenge mainstream psychology's theories about women, who are either excluded from research studies or whose experiences are assimilated to/matched against male norms (**androcentrism/the masculinist bias**). Male power and social and political oppression are screened out through **individualism**, thus playing down the **social context**. This reinforces popular gender stereotypes, contributing to women's oppression.

- Feminist psychologists also challenge psychology's claim to be an objective, value-free science. Decisions about what constitutes legitimate research are made by individual scientists within a socio-political context, making science ideological. Scientific method itself is gender-biased, concentrating on the 'subject's' behaviour, rather than its meaning, and ignoring contextual influences. These typically include a male experimenter who controls the situation.

- One consequence of the **reification** of concepts such as personality and intelligence is enforced sterilisation and abortions among various groups of women. Another is the use of the army alpha and beta tests to justify restricting immigration to the USA in the 1920s and 30s. Psychologists have a responsibility to make their values explicit about important social and political issues, and failure to do so may contribute to discrimination and oppression.

- Tavris argues that it is normal for women to feel abnormal. An example is the proposal to include **masochistic personality** within DSM-111-R. Although not intended to apply to women exclusively, changing the disorder from a psychosexual to a general personality disorder effectively made 'feminine' behaviour psychopathological. Similarly, whilst men's problems are usually explained in terms of external influences beyond their control, women's problems are attributed to internal factors, such as hormones.

- Wilson claims that men's success in commerce and academic life is due to their hormonally-determined dominance, and women who are successful may have masculinised brains. Using psychometric test results, he argues that men and women differ in terms of mental abilities, motivation, personality, and values, which are based in biology.

- According to Denmark *et al.*, gender bias is found at all stages of the **research process**. The last stage (conclusion formulation) is related to **theory construction**. Levinson *et al.*'s, Erikson's, and Kohlberg's theories all claim to present **universal** accounts of development. In fact, they are based on all-male samples and describe the world from male perspectives. Freud's psychoanalytic theory is also 'phallocentric'.

- **Cross-cultural psychology** is concerned both with behavioural variability between cultural groups and behavioural universals. It also helps to correct **ethnocentrism**. Historically, psychology has been dominated by white, middle class American males, who constitute the core of psychology's **First World**. The USA exports psychological knowledge to the rest of the world, including **Second World** countries, which are also producers. **Third World** countries are almost exclusively importers.

- American researchers and participants share a lifestyle and value system which differ from those of both most other North Americans and the rest of the world's population. Yet the research findings are applied to **people in general**, disregarding culture's relevance (the **Anglocentric/Eurocentric bias**). Cross-cultural psychologists take cultural background to be the crucial **independent variable**.

- Culture is the human-made part of the environment, comprising both **objective** and **subjective** aspects. When cross-cultural researchers compare national cultures, they fail to recognise the great diversity often found **within** them, implying that national cultures are free of conflict and dissent.

- Cultural differences can be assessed in terms of three major **cultural syndromes**, namely, **cultural complexity**, **individualism–collectivism**, and **tight vs. loose cultures**. Whilst members of every culture display both individualism and collectivism, the relative emphasis in the West is towards the former, and in the East towards the latter. This also applies to capitalist and socialist politico-economic systems respectively.

- The distinction between culture-specific and universal behaviour corresponds to the **emic–etic distinction**. When Western psychologists study non-Western cultures, they often use research tools which are emic for them but an **imposed etic** for the culture being studied. This involves imposition of the researcher's own cultural biases and theoretical framework, producing distortion of the phenomenon under investigation.

- Cross-cultural research allows researchers to examine the influence of their own beliefs and assumptions, and to appreciate the impact of situational factors on behaviour. It also allows separation of the effects of variables that may usually be confounded within the researchers' own cultures. Only by doing cross-cultural research can Western psychologists be sure that their theories and research findings are relevant outside their own cultural contexts.

ETHICAL ISSUES IN PSYCHOLOGY

Introduction and overview

6

In Chapter 4, it was noted that one of psychology's unique features is that people are both the investigators and the subject matter. This means that the 'things' studied in a psychological investigation are capable of thoughts and feelings. Biologists and medical researchers share this problem of subjecting living, sentient things to sometimes painful, stressful or strange and unusual experiences.

Just as Orne (1962) regards the psychological experiment as primarily a *social situation* (which raises questions of objectivity: see Chapter 4), so every psychological investigation is an *ethical situation* (raising questions of propriety and responsibility). Similarly, just as *methodological* issues permeate psychological research, so do *ethical* issues. For example, the *aims* of psychology as a science (see Chapters 1 and 4) concern what is *appropriate* as much as what is *possible*. Social psychology's use of stooges to deceive naïve participants, and the surgical manipulation of animals' brains in biopsychology are further examples of the essential difference between the study of the physical world and that of humans and non-humans. What psychologists can and cannot do is determined by the effects of the research on those being studied, as much as by what they want to find out.

However, psychologists are *practitioners* as well as scientists and investigators. They work in practical and clinical settings where people with psychological problems require help (see Chapter 1). Whenever the possibility of *changing* people arises, ethical issues also arise, just as they do in medicine and psychiatry. This chapter looks at the ethical issues faced by psychologists as scientists/investigators, both of humans and non-humans, and as practitioners.

Codes of conduct and ethical guidelines

Whilst there are responsibilities and obligations common to both the scientist and practitioner roles, there are also some important differences. These are reflected in the *codes of conduct* and *ethical guidelines* published by the major professional bodies for psychologists – the British Psychological Society (BPS) and the American Psychological Association (APA).

The *Code of Conduct for Psychologists* (BPS, 1985: see Figure 6.1) applies to both the major areas of research and practice, and there are additional documents designed for the two areas separately. The *Ethical Principles for Conducting Research with Human Participants* (BPS, 1990, 1993) and the *Guidelines for the Use of Animals in Research* (BPS and the Committee of the Experimental Psychological Society, 1985) obviously apply to the former, whilst, for example, the *Guidelines for the Professional Practice of Clinical Psychology* (BPS, 1983) apply to the latter.

The BPS's *Ethical Principles for Conducting Research with Human Participants* (for the rest of this chapter abbreviated to '*Ethical Principles*') identifies several guiding principles, the most important being *consent/informed consent, withdrawal from the investigation, deception, protection of participants, debriefing,* and *confidentiality*.

EXERCISE 1

Do you think it is necessary for psychologists to have written codes of conduct and ethical guidelines? What do you consider to be their major functions?

Psychologists as scientists/investigators

The problem of ethics in psychological research is daunting (Gale, 1995). Guidelines are difficult to apply in a hard-and-fast way in any particular research context. Most journals *assume* that researchers have considered ethical issues, rather than requiring

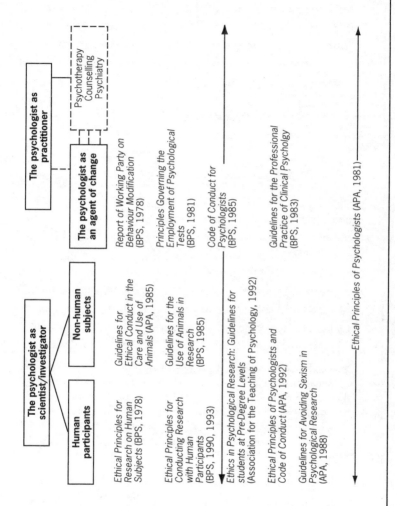

Figure 6.1 *Major codes of conduct/ethical guidelines published by the British Psychological Society (BPS) and the American Psychological Association (APA)*

formal statements to that effect. The fact that both the BPS and APA codes are periodically reviewed and revised indicates that at least some aspects do not depend on absolute or universal ethical truths (Gale, 1995). Guidelines need to be updated in light of the changing social and political context of psychological research. For example, new issues, such as sexual behaviour in the context of AIDS, might highlight new ethical problems, and, more importantly, changing views about the nature of individual rights will call into question the extent to which psychological research respects or is insensitive to such rights.

Human participants

Figure 6.1 shows that the 1978 *Ethical Principles* used the term 'subject', whilst later documents use 'participant'. Gale (1995) believes that this reflects a genuine shift in how the individual is perceived within psychology, from object (a more appropriate term than 'subject') to person. In part, this change can be attributed to the influence of *feminist* psychologists (see Chapters 4 and 5), who have also helped to bring about the removal of sexist language from BPS and APA journals as a matter of policy.

The introduction to the *Ethical Principles* (1993) states that:

'**Psychological investigators are potentially interested in all aspects of human behaviour and conscious experience. However, for ethical reasons, some areas of human experience and behaviour may be beyond the reach of experiment, observation or other form of psychological investigation. Ethical guidelines are necessary to clarify the conditions under which psychological research is acceptable**' [paragraph 1.2].

Psychologists are urged to encourage their colleagues to adopt the Principles and ensure that they are followed by all researchers whom they supervise (including *all* students, GCSE, A/AS level, undergraduate and beyond):

'**In all circumstances, investigators must consider the ethical implications and psychological consequences for the participants in their research. The essential principle is that the investigation should be** considered from the standpoint of all participants; foreseeable threats to their psychological well-being, health, values or dignity should be eliminated' [paragraph 2.1].

EXERCISE 2

In the above quote from paragraph 2.1, what do you understand by '... threats to their psychological well-being, health, values and dignity ... '? Try to identify examples of research studies which have breached this principle.

Consent, informed consent and the right to withdraw

According to the *Ethical Principles*:

'Participants should be informed of the objectives of the investigation and all other aspects of the research which might reasonably be expected to influence their willingness to participate – only such information allows *informed consent* to be given [paragraph 3.1] ... Special care needs to be taken when research is conducted with detained persons (those in prison, psychiatric hospital, etc.), whose ability to give free informed consent may be affected by their special circumstances' [paragraph 3.5].

'Investigators must realise that they often have influence over participants, who may be their students, employees or clients: this relationship must not be allowed to pressurise the participants to take part or remain in the investigation' [paragraph 3.6].

In relation to paragraph 3.6, it is standard practice in American universities for psychology students to participate in research as part of their course requirements (see Chapter 4, page 110). Whilst they are free to choose which research to participate in, they are *not* free to opt out.

Box 6.1 *Is there more to informed consent than being informed?*

Although informed consent clearly requires being informed of the procedure, participants will not have full knowledge until they have *experienced* it. Indeed, there is no guarantee that the investigators fully appreciate the procedure without undergoing it themselves. In this sense, it is difficult to argue that full prior knowledge can ever be guaranteed. How much information should be given beforehand, how much information can young children, elderly people, infirm or disabled people, or those in emotional distress be expected to absorb?

Even if a potential participant fulfils this 'informational' criterion of consent, the status of the experimenter, the desire to please others and not let them down, the desire not to look foolish by insisting on withdrawing when an experiment is already underway, all seem to detract from the idea that the participant is truly choosing *freely* in a way that is assumed by the *Ethical Principles*.
(From Gale, 1995)

Milgram's obedience experiments

Milgram's obedience experiments (1963, 1965) were ethically controversial. Baumrind (1964) accused Milgram of failing to protect his participants from the stress and emotional conflict they experienced. ✗ moral implications

---

EXERCISE 3

How did Milgram respond to Baumrind's criticism and was this a justifiable defence?

Although Milgram, arguably, met Baumrind's original criticism, it does not remove the charge of *deception* (a feature of much social psychological research). If participants were deceived as to the study's true purpose (which they unquestionably were), they could not give informed consent (see below).

Box 6.2   *Zimbardo et al.'s prison simulation experiment and informed consent*

Like Milgram's experiments, this is often cited as an example of ethically unacceptable research. However, in Zimbardo's (1973) words:
'The legal counsel of Stanford University was consulted, drew up a formal 'informed consent' statement and told us of work, fire, safety and insurance requirements we had to satisfy (which we

did). The 'informed consent' statement signed by every participant specified that there would be an invasion of privacy, loss of
some civil rights and harassment. Neither they, nor we, however,
could have predicted in advance the intensity and extent of
these aspects of the prison experience. We did not, however,
inform them of the police arrests, in part, because we did not
secure final approval from the police until minutes before they
decided to participate and, in part, because we did want the
mock arrests to come as a surprise. This was a breach, by omission, of the ethics of our informed consent contract. The staff of
the university's Student Health Department was alerted to our
study and prior arrangements made for any medical care which
might be required.'
'Approval was officially sought and received in writing from the
sponsoring agency ONR [see Box 3.1, pages 66–67], the Psychology Department and the University Committee of Human
Experimentation'.

Zimbardo *et al.*'s study was planned to last for two weeks but was
abandoned after six days because of the prisoners' distress. Why
didn't Milgram call a halt to *his* experiments when he saw how
much distress his 'teachers' were experiencing? This relates to the
issue of *withdrawal from the investigation*:

' ... investigators should make plain to the participants their right to
withdraw from the study at any time, regardless of any payment or
other inducement offered ... [paragraph 6.1]. In the light of experience of the investigation, or as a result of debriefing [see below],
participants have the right to withdraw their consent retrospectively
and to require their own data (including any recordings) to be
destroyed' [paragraph 6.2].

Milgram flagrantly contravened this principle. Each time a participant expressed the wish to stop giving shocks he or she was
urged to continue, with the prods and prompts becoming
increasingly harsh (Coolican, 1990).

An APA ethics committee investigated Milgram's research
shortly after its first publication (during which time Milgram's
APA membership was suspended), and eventually found it ethi-

cally acceptable (Colman, 1987). In 1965, Milgram was awarded the prize for outstanding contribution to social psychological research by the American Association for the Advancement of Science.

Deception

The *Ethical Principles* state that:

> 'Intentional deception of the participants over the purpose and general nature of the investigation should be avoided whenever possible. Participants should never be deliberately misled without extremely strong scientific or medical justification. Even then there should be strict controls and the disinterested approval of independent advisors' [paragraph 4.2].

The decision that deception is necessary should only be taken after determining that alternative procedures avoiding concealment or deception are unavailable, ensuring that the participants will be *debriefed* at the earliest opportunity, and consulting on how the withholding of information and deliberate deception will be received.

Some cases of deception are less serious than others. Perhaps most serious are those likely to affect the participant's *self-image*, particularly self-esteem, which is why Milgram's and Zimbardo *et al.*'s studies were so controversial. Arguably, the most potentially damaging deception goes on in social psychological research, where people are most likely to learn things about themselves *as people*. This will be of much greater emotional significance than, say, one's ability to perceive, remember or solve problems.

A form of deception used almost exclusively in social psychology is the stooge (or confederate) who (usually) pretends to be another participant (as in Milgram's experiments). An elaborate 'staging' of events occurs into which the naïve participant has to fit, without realising that any pretence is being staged.

EXERCISE 4

Drawing on field experiments such as Piliavin *et al.*'s (1969) 'New York subway' study, weigh up their *methodological advantages* (compared with laboratory experiments) against their *ethical disadvantages* (compared with laboratory experiments). Regarding the latter, try focusing on the relationship between deception and debriefing. Repeat this, using examples of *naturalistic observation* and the principle of *invasion of privacy*.

Can deception ever be justified?

Assuming it is important to understand the processes involved in obedience (the *end*), can deception be justified as a *means* of studying it, and even if it can, is it a *sufficient* justification?

Box 6.3 *How do participants feel about being deceived?*

- Mannucci (1977, cited in Milgram, 1992) asked 192 laypeople about ethical aspects of psychology experiments. They regarded deception as a relatively minor issue, and were far more concerned about the quality of the experience they would undergo as participants.
- Most participants deceived in Asch's conformity experiments were very enthusiastic and expressed their admiration for the elegance and significance of the experimental procedure (Milgram, 1992).
- In defence of his own obedience experiments, Milgram (1974) reports that his participants were all thoroughly debriefed. This involved receiving a comprehensive report which detailed the procedure and results of all the experiments, and a follow-up questionnaire concerning their participation. More specifically, the 'technical illusions' (a morally neutral term Milgram prefers to the morally biased 'deception') are justified because they are in the end accepted and endorsed by those who are exposed to them:

  'The central moral justification for allowing a procedure of the sort used in my experiment is that it is judged acceptable by those who have taken part in it. Moreover, it was the salience of this fact throughout that constituted the chief moral warrant for the continuation of the experiments' (Milgram, 1974).

- In a review of studies focusing on the ethical acceptability of deception experiments, Christensen (1988) reports that, as long as deception is not extreme, participants don't seem to mind. Christensen suggests that the widespread use of mild forms of deception is justified, first because no one is apparently harmed, and second, because there seem to be few, if any, acceptable alternatives.

- Among 255 university psychology students, those who had been deceived at least once while participating in psychological research were significantly more likely to expect to be deceived again compared with those who had not been deceived (Krupat & Garonzik, 1994). The experience of being deceived does *not*, however, have a significant impact on their evaluation of other aspects of participation, such as enjoyment and interest, and consistent with Christensen and Mannucci's findings, previously deceived participants were not particularly upset at the prospect of being deceived again. Indeed, those who had been deceived at least once said they would be *less* upset at being lied to or misled again.

Protection of participants

'Investigators have a primary responsibility to protect participants from physical and mental harm during the investigation. Normally, the risk of harm must be no greater than in ordinary life, i.e. participants should not be exposed to risks greater than or additional to those encountered in their normal life styles' [paragraph 8.1].

EXERCISE 5

Try to identify experiments in which participants have been exposed to harmful (painful or aversive) stimuli. What safeguards are there for participants in such cases?

Debriefing (together with *confidentiality* and the *right to withdraw*) represents a major means of protecting participants where emotional suffering has occurred. Participants must also be protected from the stress that might be produced by disclosing highly personal and private information. They must be reassured that they are *not* obliged to answer such questions.

Debriefing

According to Aronson (1988):

'The experimenter must take steps to ensure that subjects leave the experimental situation in a frame of mind that is at least as sound as it was when they entered. This frequently requires post-experimental 'debriefing' procedures that require more time and effort than the main body of the experiment'.

Where no undue suffering is experienced, but participants are deceived regarding the real purpose of the experiment:

'the investigator should provide the participant with any necessary information to complete their understanding of the nature of the research. The investigator should discuss with the participants their experience of the research in order to monitor any unforeseen negative effects or misconceptions' [paragraph 5.1].

However:

'some effects which may be produced by an experiment will not be negated by a verbal description following the research. Investigators have a responsibility to ensure that participants receive any necessary de-briefing in the form of active intervention before they leave the research setting' [paragraph 5.3].

This is more like a 'therapeutic' measure than just 'good manners'. Examples of this second kind of debriefing (which also incorporates the first) can be found in both the Zimbardo *et al.* and Milgram experiments.

Box 6.4 *Some examples of 'therapeutic' debriefing*

● Following Zimbardo *et al.*'s experiment, there were group and individual de-briefing sessions. All participants returned post-experimental questionnaires several weeks later, several months later, and at yearly intervals. Many submitted retrospective diaries and personal analyses of the effects of their participation. Most subsequently met with the investigators singly or in small groups, or discussed their reactions by telephone:

'We are sufficiently convinced that the suffering we observed and were responsible for, was stimulus-bound and did not extend beyond the confines of the basement prison' (Zimbardo, 1973).

- In Milgram's experiments, a very thorough debriefing ('dehoax') was carefully carried out with all participants during which they: (i) were reunited with the unharmed actor/victim, (ii) were assured that no shock had been delivered, and (iii) had an extended discussion with Milgram. Obedient participants were assured that their behaviours were entirely normal and their feelings of conflict and tension were shared by others, whilst defiant participants were supported in their decisions to disobey the experimenter. One year after the experiments, an impartial psychiatrist interviewed 40 participants, several of whom had experienced extreme stress. None showed any signs of having been psychologically harmed or having suffered traumatic reactions.

Debriefing also provides the experimenter with an opportunity to acquire additional information about the topic under investigation, so the experiment can become an educational experience for participants (Aronson, 1988). In addition, the experimenter can determine to what extent the procedure worked:

'and find out from the one person who knows best (the subject) how the procedure might be improved. In short, the prudent experimenter regards subjects as colleagues – not as objects' (Aronson, 1988).

Confidentiality

'Subject to the requirements of legislation, including the Data Protection Act, information obtained about a participant during an investigation is confidential unless otherwise agreed in advance ... Participants in psychological research have a right to expect that information they provide will be treated confidentially, and, if published, will not be identifiable as theirs' [paragraph 7.1].

Apart from the ethical considerations, a purely pragmatic argument for guaranteeing anonymity is that members of the public would soon stop volunteering if their identities were disclosed without their permission. If participants have been seriously deceived, they have the right to witness destruction of any such records they don't wish to be kept. Results are usually made anonymous as early as possible by use of a letter/number instead of name (Coolican, 1994).

In special circumstances, the investigator might contravene the confidentiality rule. For example, where there are clear or direct dangers to human life, as in participant observation of gang life where a serious crime is planned, or a psychiatrist's patient plans to kill him or herself:

> 'The ethical principles involved here are broader than those involved in conducting scientific research' (Coolican, 1994).

Widening the ethical debate: protecting the individual versus harming the group

So far, the discussion of the ethics of psychological research has focused on the vulnerability of individual participants, and psychologists' responsibilities to ensure that they do not suffer in any way from their experience of participating. Whilst 'protection of participants' is one of the specific principles included in the *Ethical Principles*, *all* the principles (informed consent, avoidance of deception and so on) are designed to prevent any harm coming to the participant, or the avoidance of overt 'sins' (Brown, 1997).

As important as this is, little attention is paid to errors of omission or covert expressions of damaging assumptions, attitudes and values which are, often unconsciously, helping to shape the research questions (see Chapters 4 and 5). Whilst individual participants may be protected from overt harm, the *social groups* to which they belong (and which they represent in the research context) may be harmed as a consequence of the research findings.

EXERCISE 6

Re-read Chapter 5. Try to identify some fundamental values and biases that are potentially damaging to particular social groups. In what ways are these values/ biases harmful to these groups?

Box 6.5 *The ethics of ethical codes: underlying assumptions*

According to Brown (1997), one core assumption underlying ethical codes is that what psychologists do as researchers, clinicians, teachers and so on is basically harmless and inherently valuable because it is based on 'science' (defined as *positivism*: see Chapter 4). Consequently, it is possible for a psychologist to conduct technically ethical research but still do great harm. For example, a researcher can adhere strictly to 'scientific' research methodologies, get technically adequate informed consent from participants (and not breach any of the other major prescribed principles), but still conduct research which claims to show the inferiority of a particular group. Because it is conducted according to 'the rules' (both methodological and ethical), the question of whether it is ethical in the broader sense to pursue such matters is ignored.

For example, neither Jensen (1969) nor Herrnstein (1971) was ever considered by mainstream psychology to have violated psychology's ethics by the questions they asked regarding the intellectual inferiority of African Americans. Individual black participants were not harmed by being given IQ tests, and might even have found them interesting and challenging. However, the way the findings were interpreted and used:

'weakened the available social supports for people of colour by stigmatising them as genetically inferior, thus strengthening the larger culture's racist attitudes. Research ethics as currently construed by mainstream ethics codes do not require researchers to put the potential for this sort of risk into their informed consent documents' (Brown, 1997).

Jensen's and Herrnstein's research (highlighted by Herrnstein & Murray, in '*The Bell Curve*', 1994) has profoundly harmed black Americans. Ironically, the book has received much *methodological criticism*, but only black psychologists (such as Hilliard, 1995, and Sue, 1995) have raised the more fundamental question of whether simply conducting such studies might be ethically dubious. As Brown observes:

'To ask this question about the risks of certain types of inquiry challenges science's hegemony as the source of all good in psychology'.

Herrnstein and Murray, Rushton (1995), Brand (cited in Richards, 1996b) and others, like the Nazi scientists of the 1930s, claim that the study of race differences is a purely 'objective' and 'scientific' enterprise (Howe, 1997).

If it is thought unethical to deceive individual black or female participants about the purposes of some particular study, but ethically acceptable to use the results to support the claim that blacks or women are genetically inferior, then this narrow definition of ethics makes it an ineffective way of guiding research into socially sensitive issues (Howitt, 1991). Formal codes continue to focus narrowly on risks to the individual participant, in the specific context of the investigation, but neglect questions about the risks to the group to which the participant belongs.

'As long as research ethics avoid the matter of whether certain questions ethically cannot be asked, psychologists will conduct technically ethical research that violates a more general ethic of avoiding harm to vulnerable populations' (Brown, 1997).

Protecting the individual versus benefiting society

If the questions psychologists ask are limited and shaped by the values of individual researchers, they are also limited and shaped by considerations of *methodology* (what it is *possible* to do, practically, when investigating human behaviour and experience). For example, in the context of intimate relationships, Brehm (1992) claims that, by its nature, the laboratory experiment is extremely limited in the kinds of questions it allows psychologists to investigate.

Conversely, and just as importantly, there are certain aspects of behaviour and experience which *could* be studied experimentally, although it would be unethical to do so, such as 'jealousy between partners participating in laboratory research' (Brehm, 1992). Indeed:

'all types of research in this area involve important ethical dilemmas. Even if all we do is to ask subjects to fill out questionnaires describing their relationships, we need to think carefully about how this research experience might affect them and their partner' (Brehm, 1992).

So, what it may be *possible* to do may be *unacceptable*, but equally, what may be *acceptable* may not be *possible*. However, just as focusing on protection of individual participants can work to the detriment of whole groups (see above), so it can discourage psychologists from carrying out *socially meaningful* research (what Brehm, 1992, calls the *ethical imperative*) which, potentially, may improve the quality of people's lives. Social psychologists in particular have a *two-fold* ethical obligation, to individual participants *and* to society at large (Myers, 1994). This relates to discussion of psychology's *aims* as a science (see Chapters 1 and 4). Similarly, Aronson (1992) argues that social psychologists are:

> 'obligated to use their research skills to advance our knowledge and understanding of human behaviour for the ultimate aim of human betterment. In short, social psychologists have an ethical responsibility to the society as a whole'.

Talking about the aim of 'human betterment' raises important questions about basic *values*. It opens out the ethical debate in such a way that values must be addressed and recognised as part of the research process (something advocated very strongly by feminist psychologists: see above and Chapter 5).

EXERCISE 7

Before reading on, try to think of some examples of how research findings that you are familiar with might be used to benefit *people in general.* You may find it useful to focus on social psychology.

Box 6.6 *An example of the benefits of social psychological research*

In many bystander intervention studies (e.g. Latané & Darley, 1968), people are deceived into believing that an 'emergency' is taking place. Many of Latané and Darley's participants were very distressed by their experiences, especially those in the experiment in which they believed another participant was having an epileptic fit. Yet when asked to complete a post-experimental questionnaire (which followed a very careful debriefing), *all* said they believed the deception was justified and would be willing to participate in similar experiments again. None reported any feelings of anger towards the experimenter.

Beaman *et al.* (1978) built on these earlier experiments. They used a lecture to inform students about how bystanders' refusals to help can influence both one's interpretation of an emergency and feelings of responsibility. Two other groups of students heard either a different lecture or no lecture at all. Two weeks later, as part of a different experiment in a different location, the participants found themselves (accompanied by an unresponsive stooge) walking past someone who was slumped over or sprawled under a bike. Of those who had heard the lecture about helping behaviour, 50 per cent stopped to offer help compared with 25 per cent who had not.

This suggests that the results of psychological research can be used to make us more aware of influences on behaviour, making it more likely that we will act differently armed with that knowledge from how we might otherwise have done. In the case of bystander intervention, this 'consciousness-raising' is beneficial in a tangible way to the person who is helped. Being more sensitive to the needs of others and feeling satisfied by having helped another person, may also be seen as beneficial to the helper.

The 'double obligation dilemma'

The dilemma faced by social psychologists (regarding their obligations to society and individual participants) is greatest when investigating important areas such as conformity, obedience and bystander intervention (Aronson, 1992). In general, the more important the issue, (i) the greater the potential benefit for society, and (ii) the more likely an individual participant is to experience distress and discomfort. This is because the more important the issue, the more essential the use of *deception* (or 'technical illusion') becomes.

Psychologists want to know how people are likely to behave if they found themselves in that situation *outside the laboratory*. This raises several crucial *methodological* questions (such as experimental realism, external validity or mundane realism).

However, the key *ethical* issue hinges on the fact that the use of deception *both* contributes enormously (and perhaps irreplaceably) to our understanding of human behaviour (helping to satisfy the obligation to society), and at the same time significantly increases individual participants' distress (detracting from the responsibility to protect individuals).

Box 6.7 *Some proposed solutions to the 'double obligation dilemma'*

- Having accepted that, under certain circumstances, deception is permissible, most psychologists still advocate that it should not be used unless it is considered *essential* (Milgram, 1992; Aronson, 1992). This is consistent with the *Ethical Principles*.

- Aronson (1992) advocates a *cost–benefit analysis*: weighing how much 'good' (benefits to society) will derive from doing the research against how much 'bad' will happen to the participants.

- Milgram (1992) believes that if the experimental creation of stress or conflict were excluded on principle, and only studies which produced positive emotions were allowed, this would produce

  '... a very lopsided psychology, one that caricatured rather than accurately reflected human experience'.

- Traditionally, the most deeply informative experiments in social psychology include those examining how participants resolve *conflicts*, such as Asch's (1952) studies of conformity (truth versus conformity), Latané and Darley's bystander intervention studies (getting involved in another's troubles versus not getting involved), and Milgram's own obedience experiments (internal conscience versus external authority).

- Two compromise solutions to the problem of not being able to obtain informed consent are *presumptive consent* (of 'reasonable people') and *prior general consent*. In the former, the views of many people are obtained about an experimental procedure's acceptability. These people would not participate in the actual experiment (if it went ahead), but their views could be taken as evidence of how people in general would react to participation.

  Prior general consent could be obtained from people who might, subsequently, serve as experimental participants. Before volunteering to join a pool of research volunteers, people would be explicitly told that sometimes participants are misinformed about a study's true purpose and sometimes experience emotional stress. Only those agreeing would be chosen (Milgram, 1992). This is a compromise solution, because people would be giving their 'informed consent' (a) well in advance of the actual study, (b) only in a very general way, and (c) without knowing what specific manipulations/deceptions will be used in the particular experiment in which they participate. It seems to fall somewhere between 'mere' consent and full 'informed consent' (and could be called *semi-* or *partially informed consent*).

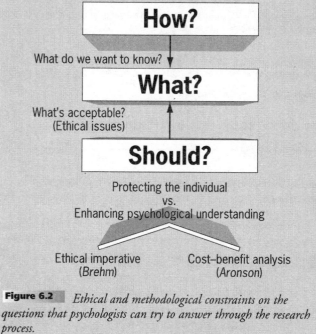

Figure 6.2 *Ethical and methodological constraints on the questions that psychologists can try to answer through the research process.*

Non-human subjects

The BPS Scientific Affairs Board published its *Guidelines for the Use of Animals in Research* (1985), in conjunction with the Committee of the Experimental Psychological Society. It offers a checklist of points which investigators should carefully consider when planning experiments with living non-humans. Researchers have a general obligation to:

> 'avoid, or at least to minimise, discomfort to living animals … discuss any future research with their local Home Office Inspector and colleagues who are experts in the topic … seek … widespread advice as to whether the likely scientific contribution of the work … justifies the use of living animals, and whether the scientific point they wish to make may not be made without the use of living animals' [BPS, 1985].

This raises two fundamental questions: (a) how do we know non-humans suffer? and (b) what goals can ever justify subjecting them to pain and suffering?

How do we know that non-humans suffer?

EXERCISE 8

Identify examples of experiments involving non-humans in which they suffered pain and distress. Try to specify *in what ways* suffering occurred.

Box 6.8 *Some criteria for judging non-human suffering*

- Disease and injury are generally recognised as major causes of suffering. Consequently, experiments like Brady's (1958) 'executive monkey' experiments would probably not even be debated in the current climate (Mapstone, 1991). Brady attached pairs of monkeys to an apparatus which gave electric shocks, such that one monkey (the 'executive': see Figure 6.3) could prevent the shock by pressing a lever but the other could not. The former developed ulcers and eventually died.

Figure 6.3

- Even if we are sure that non-humans are not suffering physically, their confinement might cause mental suffering not affecting their external condition (Dawkins, 1980). For example, apparently healthy zoo and farm animals often show bizarre behaviours.
- We must *find out* about non-human suffering by careful observation and experimentation. Because different species have different requirements, lifestyles, and, perhaps, emotions, we cannot assume that we know about their suffering or well-being without studying them species by species (Dawkins, 1980).

Drawing on the Institute of Medical Ethics (IME) Working Party's report (Haworth, 1992), Bateson (1986, 1992) has proposed criteria for assessing animal suffering, including:

- possessing receptors sensitive to noxious or painful stimulation, and
- having brain structures comparable to the human cerebral cortex.

Bateson (1992) tentatively concludes that insects probably do not experience pain, whereas fish and octopi probably do. However, the boundaries between the presence and absence of pain are 'fuzzy'.

EXERCISE 9

Try to formulate arguments for and against the use of non-humans in research. This should not be confined to *psychological* research, since much of the debate takes place in relation to medicine, pharmacology and so on.

How can we justify experiments with non-humans?

The question of suffering wouldn't arise if non-humans were not being used in experiments in the first place. According to Gray (1987), the main justifications for non-human experimentation are the pursuit of scientific knowledge and the advancement of medicine.

To justify the use of non-humans, especially when very stressful procedures are used, the research must be rigorously designed and the potential results must represent a significant contribution to our knowledge of medicine, pharmacology, biopsychology or psychology as a whole. This is a safeguard against distressing research being carried out for its own sake, or at the researcher's whim.

The *Guidelines* state that if the non-humans are confined, constrained, harmed or stressed in any way, the experimenter must consider whether the knowledge to be gained justifies the procedure. Some knowledge is trivial and experiments must not be done simply because it is possible to do them. To take the executive monkeys experiments again (see Box 6.8), the medical justification (to discover why business executives develop ulcers) was insufficient to justify their continuation. The monkeys' obvious suffering superseded even the combination of scientific and medical justification. However, there are other cases where, whilst the scientific justification may be apparent, the medical justification is much less so, such as Olds & Milner's (1954) experiments where non-humans' brains are stimulated via implantation of a permanent electrode (electrical self-stimulation of the brain/ESSB).

Safeguards for non-human subjects

Whatever practical application Olds and Milner's ESSB experiments may have subsequently had (such as pain/anxiety relief in psychotics, epileptics and cancer patients), they don't seem to have been conducted with such human applications in mind. Can the scientific knowledge gained about ESSB as a very powerful positive reinforcer *on its own* justify the rats' eventual 'sacrifice'? The very least required of researchers is that the minimum of suffering is caused, both during and following any surgical procedure and by any electric shock or food deprivation, the most objected-to treatments (Gray, 1987). Rats are the most commonly used experimental subjects in psychology.

Box 6.9 *Some safeguards for non-human subjects*

- Gray (1987) claims that food deprivation is not a source of suffering, and that the rats are either fed once a day when experimentation is over, or maintained at 85 per cent of their free-feeding (*ad lib.*) body weight. Both are actually *healthier* than allowing them to eat *ad lib*. Electric shock may cause some but not *extreme* pain (based on observations of the animals' behaviour). The level permitted is controlled by the Home Office (HO) inspectors, who monitor implementation of The Animals (Scientific Procedures) Act (1986). The average level used in the UK is 0.68 milli-amperes, for an average of 0.57 seconds. This produces an unpleasant tickling sensation in humans.

- Procedures causing pain or distress are illegal, unless the experimenter holds an HO licence and relevant certificates. Even then, there should be no alternative ways of conducting the experiment without the use of aversive stimulation. Similarly, it is illegal in the UK to perform any surgical or pharmacological procedure on vertebrates without an HO licence and relevant certification. Such procedures must be performed by experienced staff.

- The *Guidelines* stress the importance of understanding *species differences* in relation to (i) caging and social environment, (ii) the stress involved in marking wild animals for identification or attaching them with radio transmitters, and (iii) the duration of food/drink deprivation. Field workers should disturb non-humans as little as possible. Even simple observation of non-humans in the wild can have marked effects on their breeding and survival.

- The number of non-humans used in laboratory experiments is declining. For example, in the UK, the Netherlands, Germany and several other European countries, the numbers have fallen by half since the 1970s (Mukerjee, 1997).

> ● The UK, Australia, Germany and several other countries require a utilitarian *cost–benefit analysis* (non-human pain, distress and death versus acquisition of new knowledge and the development of new medical therapies for humans) to be performed before any non-human experiment can proceed (Mukerjee, 1997; Rowan, 1997).

The medical justification argument

The strongest argument for non-human experiments is undoubtedly the advancement of medical knowledge and treatments. However, it is easy for *scientific* and *ethical* issues to become confused. Demonstrations of what has been achieved in a practical sense from non-human experiments represents only a *minimum* requirement for their justification. So, only if it can be convincingly shown, for example, that many drugs used in the treatment of human diseases (including anti-cancer drugs, AIDS treatments, anti-epileptic and anti-depressant drugs: Green, 1994) have been developed using non-humans and could not have been developed otherwise, can the ethical debate begin.

Box 6.10   *Are non-human experiments scientifically useful?*

The case for
- ● Non-human experiments have played a crucial role in the development of modern medical treatments, and will continue to be necessary as researchers seek to alleviate existing ailments and respond to the emergence of new diseases.
- ● The causes of and vaccines for dozens of infectious diseases, including diphtheria, tetanus, rabies, whooping cough, tuberculosis, poliomyelitis, measles, mumps, and rubella, have been determined largely through non-human experimentation. It has also led to the development of antibacterial and antibiotic drugs.
- ● Non-human research has also been vital to areas of medicine such as open-heart surgery, kidney failure and organ transplantation, diabetes, malignant hypertension, and gastric ulcers.

- There are no basic differences between the physiologies of laboratory animals and humans. Both control their internal biochemistries by releasing the same basic endocrine hormones, both send out similar chemical transmitters from neurons in the CNS and PNS, and both react in the same way to infection or tissue injury. Non-human models of disease (see below) are intended to provide a means of studying a particular procedure (such as gene therapy for cystic fibrosis).

The case against

- Through genetic manipulation, surgical intervention, or injection of foreign substances, researchers produce diseases in laboratory animals that 'model' human diseases. However, evolutionary pressures have produced innumerable subtle differences between species, and the knock-on effect of applying a stimulus to one particular organ system on the non-human's overall physiological functioning is often unpredictable and not fully understood.

- Important medical advances have been delayed because of misleading results from non-human experiments. Cancer research is especially sensitive to physiological differences between species. Rats and mice, for example, synthesise about 100 times the recommended daily allowance of vitamin C believed to help the (human) body ward off cancer.

- The stress of handling, confinement, and isolation alters a non-human's physiology, introducing a variable that makes extrapolating results to humans even more difficult. Laboratory stress can increase non-humans' susceptibility to infectious disease and certain tumours, as well as influencing hormone and antibody levels.

- Non-human experiments to test the safety of drugs are confounded by the fact that tests on different species often produce conflicting results.

(Based on Barnard & Kaufman, 1997, Botting & Morrison, 1997, and Mukerjee, 1997)

Green (1994), Carlson (1992) and many other biopsychologists believe that the potential benefits of non-human experiments is sufficient to justify their use.

Speciesism: extending the medical justification argument

According to Gray (1991), whilst most people (both experi-menters and animal rights activists) would accept the ethical principle that inflicting pain is wrong, we are sometimes faced with having to choose between different ethical principles, which may mean having to choose between human and non-human suffering. Gray believes that *speciesism* (discriminating against and exploiting animals because they belong to a particular [non-human] species: Ryder, 1990) *is* justified, and argues that:

'not only is it not wrong to give preference to the interests of one's own species, one has a duty to do so'.

Such a moral choice involves establishing a calculus (Dawkins, 1990), which pits the suffering of non-humans against the human suffering which the former's use will alleviate. For Gray (1991):

'In many cases the decision not to carry out certain experiments with animals (even if they would inflict pain or suffering) is likely to have the consequence that more people will undergo pain or suffering that might otherwise be avoided'.

One of the problems associated with the pro-speciesism argu-ment is that medical advance may only become possible after extensive development of knowledge and scientific understand-ing in a particular field (Gray, 1991). In the meantime, scientific understanding may be the only specific objective that the exper-iment can readily attain. It is at this interim stage that the suffering imposed on experimental animals will far outweigh any (lesser) suffering eventually avoided by people, and this is at the core of the decisions that must be made by scientists and ethical committees.

Psychologists as practitioners

Clinical psychologists (as well as educational psychologists, psy-chotherapists, psychiatrists, social workers, nurses, counsellors and other professionals) are concerned with bringing about *psychological change*. It is in their capacities as *agents of change* that clinical psychologists face their greatest ethical challenges (see Chapter 1).

EXERCISE 10

Consider some of the ethical issues faced by psychologists attempting to change other people's behaviours. Some are of a general nature, such as freedom versus determinism (see Chapter 2), others will overlap with ethical principles governing research (such as confidentiality and informed consent), and yet others may be specific to particular therapeutic approaches.

According to Fairbairn & Fairbairn (1987), clinical psychologists:

'must decide how they will interact with those who seek their help; for example, whether in general they will regard them as autonomous beings with rights and responsibilities, or rather as helpless individuals, incapable of rational choice'.

Fairbairn and Fairbairn argue that two quite common beliefs likely to detract from an explicit consideration of professional ethics and values in psychological practice are (a) that psychology is a value-free science, and (b) that therapists should be value-neutral or 'non-directive'.

Psychology as value-free science

Central to clinical (and counselling) psychology is the *scientist–practitioner model* of helping (Dallos & Cullen, 1990). This sees clinical psychology as being guided by, and operating within, the framework of the general scientific method (see Chapters 4 and 5). If clinical psychologists view clinical psychology as having firm foundations in positivist science, they may disregard ethics because these are not amenable to objective consideration. However, even if the psychological knowledge used in clinical practice was always the result of the application of an objective scientific method, moral questions of an interpersonal kind are bound to arise *at the point at which it is applied* (Fairbairn & Fairbairn, 1987).

This distinction between possession of knowledge and its application ('science' versus 'technology') is fundamental to any discussion of ethics, because it is related to the notion of *responsibility*. Presumably, clinical psychologists *choose* which techniques to use with clients and how to use them. The mere existence (and even the demonstrated effectiveness) of certain techniques does not *in itself* mean that they must be used. Similarly, the kind of research which clinical psychologists consider worth doing (and which then provides the scientific basis for the use of particular techniques) is a matter of choice, and reflects views regarding the nature of people and how they can be changed (see Chapter 1).

Box 6.11 *Criticisms of scientific behaviour therapy and modification*

- Because of (rather than despite) its espoused status as a value-free, applied science, behaviour therapy and modification tend to devalue and thereby dehumanise their clients by treating people for 'scientific' purposes as if they were 'organisms' as opposed to 'agents', helpless victims of forces outside their control. This criticism also applies to medical psychiatry and classical psychoanalysis, except that both see the controlling forces as being internal (organic abnormalities or intra-psychic forces, respectively) as opposed to environmental contingencies.
- Clients soon come to believe that they are abnormal, helpless and also worthless, because this is part of the culture-wide stereotype of 'mental illness' and related terms. Negative self-evaluation and passivity characterise many, if not most, mental health clients, who think and behave like passive organisms. The solution lies in helping people recover, or discover, their agency.

(Based on Trower, 1987)

Therapists as value-neutral and non-directive

If psychology as a value-free science involves not regarding or treating clients fully as human beings, this second major issue is about the therapist or psychologist functioning as something less than a complete person within the therapeutic situation. Providing help and support in a non-directive, value-free way is a tradition for psychotherapists and counsellors (Fairbairn &

Fairbairn, 1987). However, such an approach may seem to require remaining aloof and distant from the client which, in turn, may entail not treating the client with respect as a person, since this requires the therapist to recognise that the client is a person like him- or herself.

EXERCISE 11

Evaluate the claim that it is possible for therapists not to have any influence over their clients/patients.

The influence of the therapist

Adopting what is thought to be a value-free position in therapy may lead therapists to deny the importance or influence of their own moral values, which are often hidden in therapy. This kind of influence is much more subtle and covert than the coercion that can operate on hospitalised psychiatric patients – even voluntary ones. The in-patient is subjected to strong persuasion to accept the treatment recommendations of professional staff. As Davison & Neale (1994) observe:

'even a 'voluntary' and informed decision to take psychotropic medication or to participate in any other therapy regimen is often (maybe usually) less than free'.

Box 6.12 *Therapist influence in psychodynamic and behaviour therapy*

The issue of the therapist's influence on the patient/client has been central to a long-standing debate between traditional (psychodynamic) psychotherapists and behaviour therapists (who are usually clinical psychologists by training). Psychotherapists regard behaviour therapy as unacceptable (even if it works), because it is manipulative and demeaning of human dignity. By contrast, their own methods are seen as fostering the autonomous development of the patient's inherent potential, helping the patient to express his or her true self, and so on. Instead of influencers, they see themselves as 'psychological midwives', present during the birth, possessing useful skills, but there primarily to make sure that a natural process goes smoothly.

> However, this is an exaggeration and misrepresentation of both approaches. For many patients, the 'birth' would probably not happen at all without the therapist's intervention, and he or she undoubtedly influences the patient's behaviour. Conversely, behaviour therapists are at least partly successful because they establish active, cooperative relationships with the patients, who play much more active roles in the therapy than psychotherapists believe.
>
> *All* therapists, of whatever persuasion, if they are at all effective, influence their patients. Both approaches comprise a situation in which one human being (the therapist) tries to act in a way that enables another human being to act and feel differently, and this is as true of psychoanalysis as it is of behaviour therapy.
> (From Wachtel, 1977)

The crucial issue is the *nature* of the therapist's influence rather than whether or not influence occurs. One ethical issue is whether the influence is exerted in a direction that is in the patient's interest, or in the service of the therapist's needs. Another is whether the patient is fully informed about the kind of influence the therapist wishes to exert and the kind of ends being sought (the issue of *informed consent*). Therapist *neutrality* is a myth. Therapists influence their clients in subtle yet powerful ways. According to Davison & Neale (1994):

> 'Unlike a technician, a psychiatrist cannot avoid communicating and at times imposing his own values upon his patients. The patient usually has considerable difficulty in finding the way in which he would wish to change his behaviour, but as he talks to the psychiatrist his wants and needs become clearer. In the very process of defining his needs in the presence of a figure who is viewed as wise and authoritarian, the patient is profoundly influenced. He ends up wanting some of the things the psychiatrist thinks he should want'.

In the above quotation, we can add 'psychologist' and 'psychotherapist' to 'psychiatrist'.

Freedom and behavioural control

Whilst a behavioural technique such as *systematic desensitisation* is mainly limited to anxiety reduction, this can at least be seen as enhancing the patient's freedom, since anxiety is one of the greatest restrictions on freedom. By contrast, methods based on *operant conditioning* can be applied to almost any aspect of a person's behaviour. Those who use operant methods (such as the *token economy*) often describe their work rather exclusively in terms of *behavioural control*, subscribing to Skinner's (1971) view of freedom as an illusion (see Chapter 2, page 48).

Wachtel (1977) believes that, when used in institutional settings (such as with long-term schizophrenic patients in psychiatric hospitals), the token economy is so subject to abuse that its use is highly questionable. It may be justifiable if it works, and if there is clearly no alternative way of rescuing the patient from an empty and destructive existence. However, as a routine part of how society deals with deviant behaviour, this approach raises very serious ethical questions. One of these relates to the question of *power*. Like the experimental 'subject' relative to the experimenter, the patient is powerless relative to the institutional staff responsible for operating the token economy programme:

'reinforcement is viewed by many – proponents and opponents alike – as somehow having an inexorable controlling effect upon the person's behaviour and rendering him incapable of choice, reducing him to an automaton or duly wound mechanism' (Wachtel, 1977).

It is the reinforcing agent's power to physically deprive uncooperative patients of 'privileges' that is the alarming feature of the token economy (see Gross & McIlveen, 1998).

The abuse of patients by therapists

In recent years, there has been considerable criticism of psychotherapy (especially Freudian psychoanalysis), including its ethical shortcomings. Masson (1988) believes that there is an imbalance of power involved in the therapeutic relationship, and individuals who seek therapy need protection from the therapist's constant temptation to abuse, misuse, profit from and bully the client. The therapist has almost absolute emotional power over the patient and Masson catalogues many examples of patients' emotional, sexual and financial abuse at their therapists' hands.

Not surprisingly, Masson's attack has stirred up an enormous controversy. Holmes (1992) agrees with the core of Masson's (1992) argument, namely that:

> 'no therapist, however experienced or distinguished, is above the laws of the unconscious, and all should have access to supervision and work within a framework of proper professional practice'.

However, in psychotherapy's defence, Holmes points out that exploitation and abuse are by no means confined to psychotherapy: lawyers, university teachers, priests and doctors are also sometimes guilty. All these professional groups have ethical standards and codes of practice (often far more stringent than the law of the land), with disciplinary bodies which impose severe punishments (usually expulsion from the profession). We should not condemn an entire profession because of the transgressions of a small minority.

Conclusions

This chapter has considered the ethics of psychological research, with both human participants and non-human subjects, as well as ethical issues arising from the psychologist's role as a professional involved in behaviour change. Discussion of ethical issues has, in various ways, struck at the heart of psychology itself, requiring us to ask what psychology is *for*. According to Hawks (1981), prevention rather than cure should be a primary aim of psychology, enabling people to cope by themselves, without professional help, thus 'giving psychology away' to people/clients. For Bakan (1967), the significant place in society of the psychologist is more that of the teacher than expert or technician.

Summary

- Psychology's subject matter consists of sentient things with thoughts and feelings. This makes every psychological investigation an ethical situation, with research determined as much by its effects on those being studied, as by what psychologists want to find out. Clinical psychologists also face ethical issues in their roles as agents of behavioural change.

- Various codes of conduct and ethical guidelines exist to regulate psychological research with humans and non-humans, as well as the practice of clinical and other applied branches of psychology. The BPS's *Ethical Principles* identifies several guiding principles for research with human participants, including consent/informed consent and withdrawal from the investigation, deception, protection of participants, debriefing, and confidentiality.

- The fact that codes of conduct are periodically revised means that they are not based on any absolute or universal ethical truths. However, the use of 'participant' rather than 'subject' reflects a change in psychology's perception of the individual. Ethical principles apply to all professional psychologists and to all psychology students.

- One of the controversial features of Milgram's obedience experiments was **deception** of participants, thereby preventing them from giving **informed consent**. Zimbardo *et al.*'s prison experiment provided many safeguards, including an 'informed consent' statement signed by every participant, and approval was obtained from various bodies.

- Full prior knowledge (necessary for informed consent) may not be possible without having actually experienced the procedure, and this may apply to experimenters as much as participants. Even if this were possible, the **interpersonal** nature of the experimental situation makes it unlikely that participants **freely** choose to participate.

- Zimbardo *et al.* abandoned their experiment prematurely because of the prisoners' distress, but Milgram failed to do the same in response to his participants' distress. This relates to the principle of **withdrawal from the investigation**.

- Deception should only be used as a last resort and be followed by immediate debriefing. The most potentially damaging deception occurs in social psychology, where participants are most likely to learn things about themselves **as people**. Field experiments and naturalistic observation studies present their own ethical problems, which need to be weighed against their methodological advantages.

- Research indicates that participants accept deception, provided it is not extreme, and they are not deterred from participating again. Asch's and Milgram's participants expressed very positive feelings about the experiments during their debriefings, and for Milgram this justified his use of 'technical illusions'.

- Investigators have a primary responsibility to protect participants from physical and mental harm. **Debriefing**, **confidentiality** and the right to withdraw are ways of protecting participants who have suffered emotionally. Sometimes, debriefing needs to assume a 'therapeutic' form.

- Whilst ethical codes serve to protect individual participants, underlying assumptions may harm the **social groups** they represent. For example, technically ethical research (which protects individuals) may reinforce racist attitudes (thereby harming social groups). Formal codes neglect wider issues regarding the ethical acceptability of **socially sensitive research**.

- Psychological research must be **socially meaningful** (the **ethical imperative**). This applies particularly to social psychologists, such as those engaged in bystander intervention studies. Using results from earlier studies to make participants more aware of situational influences on behaviour can increase the likelihood that they will subsequently offer help.

- The dual obligation to individual participants and to society produces a dilemma regarding the use of deception. Three possible solutions are conducting a **cost–benefit analysis**, and obtaining **presumptive** or **prior general consent**.

- Two fundamental issues relating to the use of non-humans in research are how we assess their suffering, and the goals used to justify any suffering that is produced. Whilst physical suffering is obvious, mental suffering is less overt. Species need to be studied individually, but more general criteria (such as possessing pain receptors) can also be applied.

- The main justifications for non-human experimentation are the pursuit of scientific knowledge and the advancement of medicine. Safeguards exist to minimise pain and distress in experiments, include the BPS *Guidelines* and the Animals (Scientific Procedures) Act monitored by Home Office inspectors. Several countries (including the UK) require a cost–benefit analysis to be performed.

- The medical justification argument presupposes that medical benefits have actually resulted from non-human experiments. Scientific opinion is divided about this, with some researchers stressing the biological similarities between species, others stressing subtle differences which can result in misleading and conflicting results.

- Gray advocates **speciesism** by arguing that we are morally obliged to inflict pain on non-humans in order to reduce potential human suffering. This is often a long-term goal, and ethical decisions centre around justifying non-human suffering in the short-term when only scientific knowledge is achievable.

- Clinical psychologists and other **agents of change** are likely to neglect professional ethics because of the twin beliefs that psychology is a value-free science (as embodied in the **scientist–practitioner model** of helping) and that therapists should be value-neutral/'non-directive'.

- However effective a particular technique may be, clinical psychologists still **choose** which techniques to use and what research is worth doing. Behaviour therapy and modification treat people as helpless organisms, reinforcing stereotypes of the 'mentally ill' which clients then internalise, resulting in low self-esteem and passivity.

- Psychiatric in-patients are subjected to subtle coercion to accept particular treatments, and therapists may exert an even more covert influence over their clients. Whilst psychodynamic therapists have traditionally accused behaviour therapists of manipulating and dehumanising their clients/patients, **all** therapists influence their clients/patients. The crucial issue is the **nature** of that influence.

- The **token economy** is often described in terms of **behavioural control** (based on Skinner's rejection of free will). Within institutions, staff have the **power** to deprive patients of 'privileges'. There is also a power imbalance between therapists and their clients. In both situations, abuse of power may occur.

REFERENCES

ADLER, A. (1927) *The Practice and Theory of Individual Psychology*. New York: Harcourt Brace Jovanovich.

ADORNO, T.W., FRENKEL-BRUNSWICK, E., LEVINSON, J.D. & SANFORD, R.N. (1950) The Authoritarian Personality. New York: Harper & Row.

AMERICAN PSYCHIATRIC ASSOCIATION (1968) *Diagnostical and Statisitical Manual of Mental Disorders* (2nd edition). Washington, DC. American Psychiatric Association.

AMERICAN PSYCHIATRIC ASSOCIATION (1987) *Diagnostical and Statisitical Manual of Mental Disorders* (3rd edition, revised). Washington, DC. American Psychiatric Association.

AMERICAN PSYCHOLOGICAL ASSOCIATION (1981) Ethical Principles of Psychologists. *American Psychologist, 36*, 633–638.

AMERICAN PSYCHOLOGICAL ASSOCIATION (1985) *Guidelines for Ethical Conduct in the Care and Use of Animals*. Washington, DC: American Psychological Association.

AMERICAN PSYCHOLOGICAL ASSOCIATION (1992) Ethical principles of psychologists and code of conduct. *American Psychologist, 47* (12), 1597–1612.

ARONSON, E. (1988) *The Social Animal* (5th edition). New York: Freeman.

ARONSON, E. (1992) *The Social Animal* (6th edition). New York: Freeman.

ASCH, S.E. (1952) *Social Psychology*. Englewood Cliffs, NJ: Prentice Hall.

ASSOCIATION FOR THE TEACHING OF PSYCHOLOGY (1992) Ethics in psychological research: Guidelines for students at pre-degree levels. *Psychology Teaching*, 4–10, New Series, No. 1.

ATKINSON, R.L., ATKINSON, R.C., SMITH, E.E. & BEM, D.J. (1990) *Introduction to Psychology* (10th edition). New York: Harcourt Brace Jovanovich.

BAKAN, D. (1967) *On Method*. San Francisco: Jossey-Bass Inc.

BANYARD, P. (1996) Psychology and advertising. *Psychology Review, 3* (1), September, 24–27.

BANYARD, P. & HAYES, N. (1994) *Psychology: Theory and Applications*. London: Chapman & Hall.

BARGH, J.A. & PIETROMONACO, P. (1982) Automatic information processing and social perception: The influence of trait information presented outside of conscious awareness on impression formation. *Journal of Personality & Social Psychology, 43*, 437–449.

BARNARD, N.D. & KAUFMAN, S.R. (1997) Animal research is wasteful and misleading. *Scientific American*, February, 64–66.

BATESON, P. (1986) When to experiment on animals. *New Scientist, 109* (14960), 30–32.

BATESON, P. (1992) Do animals feel pain? *New Scientist, 134* (1818), 30–33.

BAUMRIND, D. (1964) Some thoughts on the ethics of research: After reading Milgram's behavioural study of obedience. *American Psychologist, 19*, 421–423.

BEAMAN, A.L., BARNES, P.J., KLENTZ, B., & MCQUIRK, B. (1978) Increasing helping rates through information dissemination: Teaching pays. *Personality & Social Psychology Bulletin, 4*, 406–411.

BEE, H. (1994) *Lifespan Development*. New York: HarperCollins.

BERNE, E (1964) *Games People Play: The Psychology of Human Relationships*. New York: Grove Press.

BERRY, J.W. (1969) On cross-cultural compatability. *International Journal of Psychology, 4*, 119–128.

BLACKMAN, D.E. (1980) Images of man in contemporary behaviourism. In A.J. Chapman and D.M. Jones (Eds) *Models of Man*. Leicester: British Psychological Society.

BODEN, M. (1980) Artificial intelligence and intellectual imperialism. In A.J. Chapman & D.M. Jones (Eds) *Models of Man*. Leicester: British Psychological Society.

BOTTING, J.H. & MORRISON, A.R. (1997) Animal research is vital to medicine. *Scientific American*, 67–79, February.

BOWLBY, J. (1969) *Attachment and Loss*. Volume 1: Attachment. Harmondsworth, Penguin.

BRADY, J.V. (1958) Ulcers in executive monkeys. *Scientific American*, 199, 95–100.

BREHM, J.W. (1966) *A Theory of Psychological Reactance*. New York: Academic Press.

BREHM, S.S. (1992) *Intimate Relationships* (2nd edition). New York: McGraw-Hill.

BREHM, S.S. & BREHM, J.W. (1981) *Psychological Reactance: A Theory of Freedom and Control*. New York: Academic Press.

BRISLIN, R. (1993) *Understanding Culture's Influence on Behaviour*. Orlando, FL: Harcourt Brace Jovanovich.

BRITISH PSYCHOLOGICAL SOCIETY (1978) Ethical principles for research on human subjects. *Bulletin of the British Psychological Society*, 31, 48–49.

BRITISH PSYCHOLOGICAL SOCIETY (1978) Report of the Working Party on Behaviour Modification. *Bulletin of the British Psychological Society*, 31, 368–390.

BRITISH PSYCHOLOGICAL SOCIETY (1981) Principles Governing the Employment of Psychological Tests. *Bulletin of the British Psychological Society,* 34, 317–318.

BRITISH PSYCHOLOGICAL SOCIETY (1983) *Guidelines for the professional practice of clinical psychology*. Leicester: British Psychological Society.

BRITISH PSYCHOLOGICAL SOCIETY (1985) A code of conduct for psychologists. *Bulletin of the British Psychological Society*, 38, 41–43.

BRITISH PSYCHOLOGICAL SOCIETY (1990) Ethical principles for conducting research with human participants. *The Psychologist*, 3 (6), 269–272.

BRITISH PSYCHOLOGICAL SOCIETY (1993) Ethical principles for conducting research with human participants (revised). *The Psychologist*, 6 (1), 33–35.

BRITISH PSYCHOLOGICAL SOCIETY & THE COMMITTEE OF THE EXPERIMENTAL PSYCHOLOGICAL SOCIETY (1985) *Guidelines for the use of animals in research*. Leicester: British Psychological Society.

BROADBENT, D.E. (1981) Non-corporeal explanations in psychology. In A.F. Heath (Ed.) *Scientific Explanation*. Oxford: Clarendon Press.

BROWN, H. (1985) *People, Groups and Society*. Milton Keynes: Open University Press.

BROWN, J.A.C. (1963) *Techniques of Persuasion: From Propaganda to Brainwashing*. Harmondsworth: Penguin.

BROWN, L.M. & GILLIGAN, C. (1992) *Meeting at the Crossroads: Women's Psychology and Girls' Development*. Cambridge, MA.: Harvard University Press.

BROWN, L.S. (1997) Ethics in psychology: Cui bono? In D. Fox & I. Prilleltensky (Eds) *Critical Psychology: An Introduction*. London: Sage.

BRUNER, J.S., GOODNOW, J.J., & AUSTIN, G.A. (1956) *A Study of Thinking*. New York: Wiley.

BURT, C. (1943) War neuroses in British children. *Nervous Child*, 2, 324–337.

CAPLAN, P.J. (1991) Delusional dominating personality disorder (DDPD). *Feminism & Psychology*, 1 (1), 171–174.

CARLSON, N.R. (1992) *Foundations of Physiological Psychology* (2nd edition). Boston: Allyn & Bacon.

CARLSON, N.R. & BUSKIST, W. (1997) *Psychology: The Science of Behaviour* (5th edition). Needham Heights, MA.: Allyn and Bacon.

CARVER, C.S. & SCHEIER, M.F. (1992) *Perspectives on Personality* (2nd edition). Boston: Allyn & Bacon.

CERNOVSKY, Z.Z (1997) A critical look at intelligence research. In D. Fox & I. Prilleltensky (Eds) *Critical Psychology: An Introduction*. London: Sage.

CHRISTENSEN, L. (1988) Deception in psychological research: When is its use justified? *Personality & Social Psychology*, 14, 665–675.

CLARK, K.E. & MILLER, G.A. (Eds 1970) *Psychology: Behavioural and Social Sciences Survey Committee*. Englewood Cliffs, NF: Prentice Hall.

COHEN, J. (1958) *Humanistic Psychology*. London: Allen & Unwin.

COLLINS, H. (1994) *Times Higher Education Supplement*, 18, 30 September.

COLMAN, A.M. (1987) *Facts, Fallacies and Frauds in Psychology*. London: Unwin Hyman.

COOLICAN, H. (1990) *Research Methods and Statistics in Psychology*. Sevenoaks: Hodder & Stoughton.

COOLICAN, H. (1994) *Research Methods and Statistics in Psychology* (2nd edition). London: Hodder & Stoughton.

COOLICAN, H., CASSIDY, T., CHERCHER, A., HARROWER J., PENNY, G., SHARP, R., WALLEY, M. & WESTBURY, T. (1996) *Applied Psychology*. London: Hodder & Stoughton.

CRICK, F. (1994) *The Astonishing Hypothesis: The Scientific Search for the Soul*. London: Simon & Schuster.

DALLOS, R. & CULLEN, C. (1990) Clinical psychology. In I. Roth (Ed.) *Introduction to Psychology*, Volume 2. Hove/E.Sussex/Milton Keynes: Open University Press/Lawrence Erlbaum Associates Ltd.

DARWIN, C.R. (1859) *The Origin of Species by Means of Natural Selection*. London: John Murray.

DAVISON, G. & NEALE, J. (1994) *Abnormal Psychology* (6th edition). New York: Wiley.

DAWKINS, M.S. (1980) The many faces of animal suffering. *New Scientist*, November 20.

DAWKINS, M.S. (1990) From an animal's point of view: Motivation, fitness and animal welfare. *Behavioural and Brain Sciences*, 13, 1–9.

DECI, E.L. (1980) *The Psychology of Self-determination*. Lexington, MA.: D.C. Heath.

DECI, E.L. & RYAN, R.M. (1987) The support of autonomy and the control of behaviour. *Journal of Personality & Social Psychology*, 53, 1024–1037.

DEESE, J. (1972) *Psychology as Science and Art*. New York: Harcourt Brace Jovanovich.

DELGADO, J.M.R. (1969) *Physical Control of the Mind*. New York: Harper & Row.

DENMARK, F., RUSSO, N.F., FRIEZE, I.H., & SECHZER, J.A. (1988) Guidelines for avoiding sexism in psychological research: A report of the ad hoc committee on nonsexist research. *American Psychologist*, 43 (7), 582–585.

DRAKELEY, R. (1997) Psychometric testing. *Psychology Review*, 3 (3), 27–29, February.

DUNSDON, M.I. (1941) A psychologist's contribution to air raid problems. *Mental Health*, 2, 37–41.

EAGLY, A.H. (1987) *Sex Differences in Social Behaviour: A Social Role Interpretation*. Hillsdale, NJ.: Erlbaum.

EISER, J.R. (1994) *Attitudes, Chaos and the Connectionist Mind*. Oxford: Blackwell.

ELLIOT, C.D., MURRAY, D.J., & PEARSON, L.S. (1979, revised 1983) *British Ability Scales*. Slough: National Foundation for Educational Research.

ELLIS, A. (1958) *Rational Psychotherapy*. California: Institute for Rational Emotive Therapy.

ERIKSON, E.H. (1950) *Childhood and Society*. New York: Norton.

ERIKSON, E.H. (1968) *Identity: Youth and Crisis*. New York: Norton.

EYSENCK, H.J. (1985) *Decline and Fall of the Freudian Empire*. Harmondsworth: Penguin.

EYSENCK, H.J. & WILSON, G.D. (1973) *The Experimental Study of Freudian Theories*. London: Methuen.

EYSENCK, M.W. & KEANE, M.J. (1995) *Cognitive Psychology: A Student's Handbook* (3rd edition). Hove: Erlbaum.

FAIRBAIRN, G. & FAIRBAIRN, S. (1987) Introduction. In S. Fairbairn & G. Fairbairn (Eds) *Psychology, ethics and change*. London: Routledge & Kegan Paul.

FAIRBAIRN, R. (1952) *Psychoanalytical Studies of the Personality*. London: Tavistock.

FANCHER, R.E. (1979) *Pioneers of Psychology*. New York: Norton.

FANCHER, R.E. (1996) *Pioneers of Psychology* (3rd edition). New York: Norton.

FLANAGAN, O.J. (1984) *The Science of the Mind*. Cambridge, Mass.: MIT Press.

FREUD, A. & BURLINGHAM, D. (1942) *Young Children in Wartime*. London: Allen & Unwin.

FREUD, S. (1900) *The Interpretation of Dreams*. London: Hogarth Press.

FREUD, S. (1914) Remembering, repeating and working through. *Standard Edition*, Volume XII. London: Hogarth Press.

FREUD, S. (1949) *An Outline of Psycho-analysis*. London: Hogarth Press.

GALE, A. (1990) *Thinking about Psychology?* (2nd edition). Leicester: British Psychological Society.

GALE, A. (1995) Ethical issues in psychological research. In A.M. Colman (Ed.) *Psychological research methods and statistics*. London: Longman.

GARDNER, H. (1983) *Frames of Mind: The Theory of Multiple Intelligences*. New York: Basic Books.

GARNHAM, A. (1991) *The Mind in Action*. London: Routledge.

GARRETT, R. (1996) Skinner's case for radical behaviourism. In W. O'Donohue & R.F. Kitchener (Eds) *The Philosophy of Psychology*. London: Sage.

GAY, P. (1988) *Freud: A Life for our Time*. London: J.M. Dent & Sons.

GELDER, M., GATH, D. & MAYON, R. (1989) *The Oxford Textbook of Psychiatry* (2nd edition). Oxford: Oxford University Press.

GEUTER, U. (1992) *The Professionalization of Psychology in Nazi Germany*. Cambridge: Cambridge University Press.

IBSON, J.J. (1950) *The Perception of the Visual World*. Boston: Houghton Mifflin.

GIDDENS, A. (1979) *Central Problems in Social Theory*. Basingstoke: Macmillan.

GILLIGAN, C. (1982) *In a Different Voice: Psychological Theory and Women's Development*. Cambridge, MA: Harvard University Press.

GILLIGAN, C. (1993) Letter to Readers (Preface) In *In A Different Voice*. Cambridge, MA.: Harvard University Press.

GLASSMAN, W.E. (1995) *Approaches to Psychology* (2nd edition). Buckingham: Open University.

GOULD, R.L. (1978) *Transformations: Growth and Change in Adult Life*. New York: Simon & Schuster.

GOULD, R.L. (1980) Transformational tasks in adulthood. In S.I. Greenspan & G.H. Pollock (Eds) *The Course of Life: Psychoanalytic Contributions Toward Understanding Personality Development*, Volume 3: *Adulthood and the Ageing Process*. Washington, DC: National Institute for Mental Health.

GOULD, S.J. (1981) *The Mismeasure of Man*. Harmondsworth: Penguin.

GRAY, J.A. (1987) The ethics and politics of animal experimentation. In H. Beloff & A.M. Colman (Eds) *Psychology Survey*, No.6. Leicester: British Psychological Society.

GRAY, J.A. (1991) On the morality of speciesism. *The Psychologist*, 4 (5), 196–198.

GREEN, S. (1994) *Principles of Biopsychology*. Sussex: Lawrence Erlbaum Associates.

GREENWALD, A.G., KLINGER M.R. & LIU, T.J. (1989) Unconscious processing of dichoptically masked words. *Memory & Cognition*, 17, 35–47.

GREGORY, R.L. (1981) *Mind in Science*. Harmondsworth: Penguin.

GROSS, R. (1995) *Themes, Issues and Debates in Psychology*. London: Hodder & Stoughton.

GROSS, R. (1996) *Psychology: The Science of Mind and Behaviour* (3rd edition). London: Hodder & Stoughton.

GROSS, R. & McILVEEN, R. (1998) *Psychology: A New Introduction*. London: Hodder & Stoughton.

GROSZ, E.A. (1987) Feminist theory and the challenge of knowledges. *Women's Studies International Forum*, 10, 475–480.

HARRÉ, R. (1989) Language games and the texts of identity. In J. Shotter & K.J. Gergen (Eds) *Texts of Identity*. London: Sage.

HARRÉ, R., CLARKE, D., & De CARLO, N. (1985) *Motives and Mechanisms: An Introduction to the Psychology of Action*. London: Methuen.

HARTLEY, J. & BRANTHWAITE, A. (1997) Earning a crust. *Psychology Review*, 3 (3), 24–26.

HAWKS, D. (1981) The dilemma of clinical practice – Surviving as a clinical psychologist. In I. McPherson & M. Sutton (Eds) *Reconstructing Psychological Practice*. London: Croom Helm.

HAWORTH, G. (1992) The use of non-human animals in psychological research: the current status of the debate. *Psychology Teaching*, 46–54. New Series, No.1.

HEATHER, N. (1976) *Radical Perspectives in Psychology*. London: Methuen.

HEBB, D.O. (1952) The effects of isolation upon attitudes, motivation and thought. *Fourth Symposium, Military Medicine, I. Defence Research Board*: Canada.

HERRNSTEIN, R.J. (1971) IQ. *Atlantic Monthly*, September, 43–64.

HERRNSTEIN, R.J. & MURRAY, C. (1994) *The Bell Curve: Intelligence and Class Structure in American Life*. New York: Free Press.

HERSKOVITS, M.J. (1955) *Cultural Anthropology*. New York: Knopf.

HILLIARD, A.G. (1995) The nonscience and nonsense of the bell curve. *Focus: Notes from the Society for the Psychological Study of Ethnic Minority Issues*, 10–12.

HOLMES, D.S. (1994) *Abnormal Psychology* (2nd edition). New York: HarperCollins.

HOLMES, J. (1992) Response to Jeffrey Masson. In W. Dryden & C. Feltham (Eds) *Psychotherapy and its Discontents*. Buckingham: Open University Press.

HOLMES, J. (1993) *John Bowlby and Attachment Theory*. London: Routledge.

HOWE, M. (1997) *IQ in Question: The Truth about Intelligence*. London: Sage.

HOWITT, D. (1991) *Concerning Psychology: Psychology Applied to Social Issues*. Milton Keynes: Open University Press.

JACOBS, M. (1992) *Freud*. London: Sage Publications.

JAHODA, G. (1978) Cross-cultural perspectives. In H. Tajfel & C. Fraser (Eds) *Introducing Social Psychology*. Harmondsworth: Penguin.

JAMES, W. (1890) *The Principles of Psychology*. New York: Henry Holt & Company.

JENSEN, A. (1969) How much can we boost IQ and scholastic achievement? *Harvard Educational Review*, 39, 1–23.

JOYNSON, R.B. (1980) Models of man: 1879–1979. In A.J. Chapman & D.M. Jones (Eds) *Models of Man*. Leicester: British Psychological Society.

JUNG, C.G. (1964) *Man and His Symbols*. London: Aldus–Jupiter Books.

KLEIN, M. (1932) *The Psychoanalysis of Children*. London: Hogarth Press.

KLINE, P. (1988) *Psychology Exposed*. London: Routledge.

KLINE, P. (1995) Personality tests. In S.E. Hampson & A.M. Colman (Eds) *Individual Differences and Personality*. London: Longman.

KOESTLER, A. (1967) *The Ghost in the Machine*. London: Pan.

KOHLBERG, L. (1969) Stage and sequence: The cognitive developmental approach to socialisation. In D.A. Goslin (Ed.) *Handbook of Socialisation Theory and Research*. Chicago: Rand McNally.

KRUPAT, E. & GARONZIK, R. (1994) Subjects' expectations and the search for alternatives to deception in social psychology. *British Journal of Social Psychology*, 33, 211–222.

KUHN, T.S. (1962) *The Structure of Scientific Revolutions*. Chicago: University of Chicago Press.

KUHN, T.S. (1970) *The Structure of Scientific Revolutions* (2nd edition). Chicago: University of Chicago Press.

LADD, G.W. & CAIRNS, E. (1996) Children: Ethnic and political violence. *Child Development*, 67, 14–18.

LAMBIE, J. (1991) The misuse of Kuhn in psychology. *The Psychologist*, 4 (1), 6–11.

LATANÉ, B. & DARLEY, J.M. (1968) Group inhibitions of bystander intervention in emergencies. *Journal of Personality and Social Psychology*, 10, 215–221.

LeFRANCOIS, G.R. (1983) *Psychology*. Belmont, CA: Wadsworth Publishing Co.

LEGGE, D. (1975) *An Introduction to Psychological Science*. London: Methuen.

LEPPER, M.R., GREENE, D., & NISBETT, R.E. (1973) Undermining children's intrinsic interest with extrinsic reward: A test of the overjustification hypothesis. *Journal of Personality & Social Psychology*, 28, 129-137.

LEVINSON, D.J., DARROW, D.N., KLEIN, E.B., LEVINSON, M.H. & McKEE, B. (1978) *The Seasons of a Man's Life*. New York: A.A. Knopf.

LORENZ, K.Z. (1966) *On Aggression*. London: Methuen.

LURIA, A.R. (1987) Reductionism. In R.L. Gregory (Ed.) *The Oxford Companion to the Mind*. Oxford: Oxford University Press.

MAPSTONE, E. (1991) Special issue on animal experimentation. *The Psychologist*, 4 (5), 195.

MASLOW, A. (1968) *Towards a Psychology of Being* (2nd edition). New York: Van Nostrand Reinhold.

MASSON, J. (1988) *Against Therapy: Emotional Tyranny and the Myth of Psychological Healing*. New York: Athaneum.

MEDAWAR, P.B. (1963) *The Art of the Soluble*. Harmondsworth: Penguin.

MILGRAM, R.M. & MILGRAM, N.A. (1976) The effect of the Yom Kippur War on anxiety level in Israeli children. *Journal of Psychology*, 94, 107–113.

MILGRAM, S. (1963) Behavioural study of obedience. *Journal of Abnormal and Social Psychology*, 67, 391–398.

MILGRAM, S. (1965) Liberating effects of group pressure. *Journal of Personality and Social Psychology*, 1, 127–134.

MILGRAM, S. (1974) *Obedience to Authority*. New York: Harper & Row.

MILGRAM, S. (1992) *The Individual in a Social World* (2nd edition). New York: McGraw-Hill.

MILLER, G.A. (1962) *Psychology: The Science of Mental Life*. Harmondsworth: Penguin.

MOGHADDAM, F.M. (1987) Psychology in the Three Worlds: As Reflected by the Crisis in Social Psychology and the Move towards Indigenous Third World Psychology. *American Psychologist*, 42, 912–920.

MOGHADDAM, F.M. & STUDER, C. (1997) Cross-cultural psychology: The frustrated gladfly's promises, potentialities and failures. In D. Fox & D. Prilleltensky (Eds) *Critical Psychology: An Introduction*. London: Sage.

MOGHADDAM, F.M., TAYLOR, D.M. & WRIGHT, S.C. (1993) *Social Psychology in Cross-cultural Perspective*. New York: W.H. Freeman & Co.

MOREA, P. (1990) *Personality: An Introduction to the Theories of Psychology*. Harmondsworth: Penguin.

MUKERJEE, M. (1997) Trends in animal research. *Scientific American*, 63, February.

MYERS, D.G. (1994) *Exploring Social Psychology*. New York: McGraw-Hill.

NEWELL, A., SHAW, J.C. & SIMON, H.A. (1958) Elements of a theory of human problem-solving. *Psychological Review*, 65, 151–166.

NEWELL, A. & SIMON, H.A. (1972) *Human Problem-Solving*. Englewood Cliffs, NJ: Prentice-Hall.

NEWMAN, M., BLACK, D. & HARRIS-HENDRIKS, J. (1997) Victims of disaster, war, violence, or homicide: Psychological effects on siblings. *Child Psychology & Psychiatry Review*, 2 (4), 140–149.

NICOLSON, P. (1995) Feminism and psychology. In J.A.Smith, R. Harre, & L. Van Langenhove (Eds) *Rethinking Psychology*. London: Sage.

NORMAN, D.A. & SHALLICE, T. (1986) Attention to action: Willed and automatic control of behaviour. In R.J. Davidson, G.E. Schwartz & D. Shapiro (Eds) *The Design of Everyday Things*. New York: Doubleday.

OLDS, J. & MILNER, P. (1954) Positive reinforcement produced by electrical stimulation of the septal area and other regions of the rat brain. *Journal of Comparative and Physiological Psychology*, 47, 419–427.

ORNE, M.T. (1962) On the social psychology of the psychological experiment – with particular reference to demand characteristics. *American Psychologist*, 17 (11), 776–783.

PACKARD, V. (1957) *The Hidden Persuaders*. New York: McKay.

PALERMO, D.S. (1971) Is a scientific revolution taking place in psychology? *Psychological Review*, 76, 241–263.

PENFIELD, W. (1947) Some observations on the cerebral cortex of man. *Proceedings of the Royal Society*, 134, 349.

PENROSE, R. (1990) *The Emperor's New Mind*. Oxford: Oxford University Press.

PERLS, F.S. (1967) Group versus individual therapy. *ETC: A Review of General Semantics*. 34, 306–312.

PIKE, K.L. (1954) Emic and etic standpoints for the description of behaviour. In K.L. Pike (Ed.) *Language in Relation to a Unified Theory of the Structure of Human Behaviour* (Prelim. edition). Glendale, CA.: Summer Institute of Linguistics.

PILIAVIN, I.M., RODIN, J. & PILIAVIN, J.A. (1969) Good Samaritanism: An underground phenomenon? *Journal of Personality and Social Psychology*, 13, 289–299.

POPPER, K. (1959) *The Logic of Scientific Discovery*. London: Hutchinson.

POPPER, K. (1972) Objective Knowledge: An Evolutionary Approach. Oxford: Oxford University Press.

PRATKANIS, A. & ARONSON, E. (1991) *Age of Propaganda: Everyday Uses and Abuses of Persuasion*. New York: Freeman.

PRATKANIS, A.R., ESKENAZI, J. & GREENWALD A.G. (1990) *What you expect is what you believe (but not necessarily what you get): On the ineffectiveness of subliminal self-help audiotapes*. Paper presented at the Western Psychological Association, Los Angeles, CA, (April).

PRINCE, J. & HARTNETT, O. (1993) From 'psychology constructs the female' to 'females construct psychology'. *Feminism & Psychology*, 3 (2), 219–224.

PRINS, H. (1995) *Offenders, Deviants or Patients?* (2nd edition) London: Routledge.

RICHARDS, A. & WOPERT, L. (1997) The Insiders' Story. *Independent on Sunday Review*, 27 September, 44–45.

RICHARDS, G. (1996a) *Putting Psychology in its Place*. London: Routledge.

RICHARDS, G. (1996b) Arsenic and old race. *Observer Review*, 5 May, 4.

RICHARDSON, K. (1991) *Understanding Intelligence*. Milton Keynes: Open University Press.

RINGEN, J. (1996) The behaviour therapist's dilemma: Reflections on autonomy, informed consent, and scientific psychology. In W. O'Donohue & R.F. Kitchener (Eds) *The Philosophy of Psychology*. London: Sage Publications.

ROGERS, C.R. (1951) *Client-Centred Therapy: Its Current Practice, Implications and Theory*. Boston: Houghton-Mifflin.

ROGERS, C.R. (1959) A theory of therapy, personality and interpersonal relationships as developed in the client-centred framework. In S. Koch (Ed.) *Psychology: A Study of Science, Volume III, Formulations of the Person and the Social Context*. New York: McGraw-Hill.

ROGERS, C.R. (1983) *Freedom to Learn in the '80s*. Columbus, OH.: Charles Merrill.

ROGOFF B. & MORELLI, G. (1989) Perspectives on children's development from cultural psychology. *American Psychologist*, 44, 343–348.

ROSE, S. (1992) *The Making of Memory: From molecule to mind*. London: Bantam Books.

ROSE, S., LEWONTIN, R.C., & KAMIN, L.J. (1984) *Not in our Genes: Biology, Ideology and Human Nature*. Harmondsworth: Penguin.

ROSENTHAL, R. (1966) *Experimenter Effects in Behavioural Research*. New York: Appleton-Century-Crofts.

ROSENTHAL, R. & FODE, K.L. (1963) The effects of experimenter bias on the performance of the albino rat. *Behavioural Science*, 8, 183–189.

ROSENTHAL, R. & JACOBSON, L. (1968) *Pygmalian in the Classroom*. New York: Holt, Rinehart, Winston.

ROSENTHAL, R. & LAWSON, R. (1961) 'A longitudinal study of the effects of experimenter bias on the operant learning of laboratory rats.' (Unpublished manuscript, Harvard University.)

ROWAN, A.N. (1997) The benefits and ethics of animal research. *Scientific American*, 64–66, February.

RUSHTON, J.P. (1995) *Race, Evolution and Behaviour*. New Brunswick, NJ: Transaction Publishers.

RYCROFT, C. (1966) Introduction: Causes and Meaning. In C. Rycroft (Ed.) *Psychoanalysis Observed*. London: Constable & Co. Ltd.

RYDER, R. (1990) Open reply to Jeffrey Gray. *The Psychologist*, 3, 403.

SCODEL, A. (1957) Heterosexual somatic preference and fantasy dependence. *Journal of Consulting Psychology*, 21, 371–374.

SHERIF, M., HARVEY, O.J., WHITE, B.J., HOOD, W.R. & SHERIF, C.W. (1961) *Inter-Group Conflict and Co-Operation: The Robber's Cave Experiment*. Norman, OK: University of Oklahoma Press.

SKINNER, B.F. (1948) *Walden Two*. New York: Macmillan.

SKINNER, B.F. (1971) *Beyond Freedom and Dignity*. New York: Knopf.

SKINNER, B.F. (1974) *About Behaviourism*. New York: Alfred Knopf.

SKINNER, B.F. (1987) Skinner on Behaviourism. In R.L. Gregory (Ed.) *The Oxford Companion to the Mind*. Oxford: Oxford University Press.

SMITH, C.U.M. (1994) You are a group of neurons. *The Times Higher Educational Supplement*, 27 May, 20–21.

SMITH, J.A., HARRÉ, R., & VAN LANGENHOVE, L. (1995) Introduction. In J.A.Smith, R. Harré, & L. Van Langenhove (Eds) *Rethinking Psychology*. London: Sage.

SMITH, P.B. & BOND, M.H. (1993) *Social Psychology Across Cultures: Analysis and Perspectives*. Hemel Hempstead: Harvester Wheatsheaf.

SMITH, P.K. & COWIE, H. (1991) *Understanding Children's Development* (2nd edition). Oxford: Basil Blackwell.

STERNBERG, R.J. (1990) *Metaphors of Mind*. Cambridge: Cambridge University Press.

STEVENS, R. (1995) Freudian theories of personality. In S.E. Hampson & A.M. Colman (Eds) *Individual Differences and Personality*. London: Longman.

STRACHEY, J. (1962–1977) *Sigmund Freud: A sketch of his life and ideas*. This appears in each volume of the Pelican Freud Library: originally written for the *Standard Edition of the Complete Psychological Works of Sigmund Freud, 1953–1974*. London: Hogarth Press.

SUE, S. (1995) Implications of the Bell curve: Whites are genetically inferior in intelligence? *Focus: Notes from the Society for the Psychological Study of Ethnic Minority Issues*, 16–17.

SULLOWAY, F.J. (1979) *Freud, Biologist of the Mind: Beyond the Psychoanalytic Legend*. New York: Basic Books.

TAVRIS, C. (1993) The mismeasure of woman. *Feminism & Psychology*, 3 (2), 149–168.

TAYLOR, R. (1963) *Metaphysics*. Englewood Cliffs, NJ: Prentice-Hall.

TEICHMAN, J. (1988) *Philosophy and the Mind*. Oxford: Blackwell.

THORNE, B. (1992) *Rogers*. London: Sage Publications.

THIBAUT, J.W. & KELLEY, H.H. (1959) *The Social Psychology of Groups*. New York: Wiley.

TOLMAN, E.C. (1948) Cognitive maps in rats and man. *Psychological Review*, 55, 189–208.

TRIANDIS, H.C. (1990) Theoretical concepts that are applicable to the analysis of ethnocentrism. In R.W. Brislin (Ed.) *Applied Cross-Cultural Psychology*. Newbury Park, CA.: Sage.

TRIANDIS, H.C. (1994) *Culture and Social Behaviour*. New York: McGraw-Hill.

TROWER, P. (1987) On the ethical bases of 'scientific' behaviour therapy. In S. Fairbairn & G. Fairbairn (Eds) *Psychology, Ethics and Change*. London: Routledge & Kegan Paul.

UDWIN, O. (1993) Children's reactions to traumatic events. *Journal of Child Psychology & Psychiatry*, 34 (2), 115–127.

UDWIN, O. (1995) Psychological intervention with war-traumatized children in Bosnia: A consultation model. *Association for Child Psychology & Psychiatry Review & Newsletter*, 17 (4), 195–200.

UNGER, R. & CRAWFORD, M. (1992) *Women and Gender: A Feminist Psychology*. New York: McGraw-Hill.

VALENTINE, E.R. (1982) *Conceptual Issues in Psychology*. London: Routledge.

VALENTINE, E.R. (1992) *Conceptual Issues in Psychology* (2nd edition). London: Routledge.

VAN LANGENHOVE, L. (1995) The theoretical foundations of experimental psychology and its alternatives. In J.A.Smith, R. Harré, & L. Van Langenhove (Eds) *Rethinking Psychology*. London: Sage.

WACHTEL, P.L. (1977) *Psychoanalysis and Behaviour Therapy: Towards an Integration*. New York: Basic Books.

WADELEY, A. (1996) Subliminal perception. *Psychology Review*, 3 (1), September.

WATSON, J.B. (1913) Psychology as the behaviourist views it. *Psychological Review*, 20, 158–177.

WATSON, J.B. (1919) *Psychology from the Standpoint of a Behaviourist*. Philadelphia: J.B. Lippincott.

WECHSLER, D. (1992) Wechsler Intelligence Scale for Children (3rd edition) UK (WISC-III-UK). *The Psychological Corporation*, Sidcup, Kent: Harcourt Brace & Co.

WEISSTEIN, N. (1993) Psychology constructs the female; or, The fantasy life of the male psychologist (with some attention to the fantasies of his friend, the male biologist and the male anthropologist). *Feminism & Psychology*, 3 (2), 195–210.

WILKINSON, S. (1991) Feminism & psychology: From critique to reconstruction. *Feminism & Psychology*, 1 (1), 5–18.

WILKINSON, S, (1997) Feminist Psychology. In D. Fox & D. Prilleltensky (Eds) *Critical Psychology: An Introduction*. London: Sage.

WILSON, G. (1994) Biology, sex roles and work. In C. Quest (Ed.) *Liberating Women from Modern Feminism*. London: Institute of Economic Affairs, Health & Welfare Unit.

WILSON, G.T., O'LEARY, K.D., NATHAN, P.E. & CLARK, L.A. (1996) *Abnormal Psychology: Integrating Perspectives*. Needham Heights, MA.: Allyn and Bacon.

WOBER, M. (1974) Towards an understanding of the Kiganda concept of intelligence. In J.W. Berry & P.R. Dasen (Eds) *Culture and Cognition*. London: Methuen.

WOLPE, J. (1958) *Psychotherapy by Reciprocal Inhibition*. Stanford, CA: Stanford University Press.

WUNDT, W. (1874) *Grundzuge der Physiologischen Psychologie*. Leipzig: Engelmann.

ZIMBARDO, P.G. (1973) On the ethics of intervention in human psychological research with special refernce to the 'Stanford Prison Experiment'. *Cognition*, 2 (2), 243–255.

ZIMBARDO, P.G. (1992) *Psychology and Life* (13th edition) New York: Harper Collins.

ZIMBARDO, P.G., BANKS, W.C., CRAIG, H. & JAFFE, D. (1973) A Pirandellian prison: The mind is a formidable jailor. *New York Times Magazine*, 8 April, 38–60.

ZIMBARDO, P.G. & LEIPPE, M. (1991) *The Psychology of Attitude Change and Social Influence*. New York: McGraw-Hill.

ZIV, A. & ISRAELI, R. (1973) Effects of bombardment on the manifest anxiety level of children living in kibbutzim. *Journal of Consulting & Clinical Psychology*, 40, 287–291.

INDEX

abnormal psychology, 9

actualising tendency (Rogers), 29

Adler, A., 22, 25, 29

Adorno, T.W., 24, 54, 77

advertising, 63, 73–76
  as a form of active social
    influence/persuasion, 63, 64
  ethics of, 75–76
  and occupational psychology, 15
  subliminal, 73–76

African Americans, 83, 152

American Association for the
  Advancement of Science, 146

American Psychiatric Association,
  123

American Psychological
  Association (APA), 140
  Committee on Nonsexist
    Research, 125
  *Ethical Principles of
    Psychologists*, 141
  *Ethical Principles of
    Psychologists and Code of
    Conduct*, 141
  *Guidelines for Avoiding Sexism
    in Psychological Research*,
    125–126, 141
  *Guidelines for Ethical Conduct
    in the Care and Use of
    Animals*, 141

analytical psychology (Jung), 25

androcentric (masculinist) bias,
  110, 117–128, 130
  and ethics, 122
  and moral development, 122
  practical consequences of,
    121–122

Anglocentric (Eurocentric) bias,
  110, 147

and ethics, 122

Animals (Scientific Procedures)
  Act, 161

anthropomorphism, 39

Aronson, E., 69, 72, 149, 150,
  154, 155, 156, 157, 158

artificial intelligence, 95

artificiality (of empirical
  methods), 111

Asch, S.E., 156

association (in advertising), 73

Association for the Teaching of
  Psychology
  *Ethics in Psychological Research:
    Guidelines for students at
    Pre-Degree Levels*, 141

associationism (and empirism), 94

Atkinson, R.L., 11

attribution theory (and
  explanations of sex
  differences), 119, 124

atypical development, 9

authoritarian personality (account
  of prejudice), 24, 54

Baganda people (Uganda), 134

Bakan, D., 170

Banyard, P., 73

Bargh, J.A., 75

Barnard, N.D., 163

Bateson, P., 159

Baumrind, D., 144

Beaman, A.L., 155

Bee, H., 82, 83

behaviour modification, 11, 12,
  20, 64
  ethical criticisms of, 166
  and the token economy, 169

behaviour therapist's dilemma,
  50–**51**

behaviour therapy, 11, 12, 20, 64
and psychotherapy, 167–168
and systematic desensitisation,
26, 168
behavioural genetics, 8
behaviourism, 1, 2–3, 4, 7, 16,
18–21, 24, 28, 32, 43, 55,
92, 94, 102, 103, 104
cognitive, 20
methodological, 16, 18, 20
practical contributions of, 20
radical, 16, 18, 21, 48, 50, 51,
55
and S–R psychology, 19
theoretical contributions of,
19–20
behaviourist manifesto (Watson),
2–3, 16, 92–93
Berkeley, Bishop, 88
Berne, E., 26
Berry, J.W., 132, 133
biofeedback, 20
biological bases of behaviour (see
biopsychology)
biopsychology, 6–7
Blackman, D.E., 16
Boden, M., 103
Bond, M.H., 128, 131, 132, 133,
135
Botting, J.H., 163
Bowlby, J., 25
brainwashing, 64, 67
Branthwaite. A., 10, 11
Brehm, J.W., 40
Brehm, S.S., 40, 153, 154, 157
Brislin, R., 133, 134, 135
British Ability Scales (BAS), 81
British Institute of Practitioners in
Advertising, 75

British Psychological Society
(BPS), 15
Code of Conduct for
Psychologists, 140, 141
Ethical Principles for Conducting
Research with Human
Participants, 140, 141,
142, 143, 144, 145, 146,
147, 148, 149, 150, 153,
154
Ethical Principles for Research on
Human Subjects, 141
Guidelines for the Professional
Practice of Clinical
Psychology, 140, 141
Guidelines for the Use of Animals
in Research, 140, 141, 158,
160, 161
Principles Governing the
Employment of Psychological
Tests 141
Report of Working Party on
Behaviour Modification 141
Broadbent, D.E., 58
Broadmoor (special hospital), 13,
44
Brody, J.V., 158
Brown, H., 66, 67
Brown, J.A.C., 69, 70, 71, 73, 76
Brown, L.M., 127
Brown, L.S., 151, 152, 153
Bruner, J.S., 95
Burlingham, D., 68
Burt, C., 68
Buskist, W., 31
bystander intervention, 154–155,
156
Cairns, E., 69
Caplan, P.J., 123

Carlson, N.R., 31, 163
Carver, C.S., 41
Cernovsky, Z.Z., 83
Certificate of Competence in
    Occupational Testing (BPS),
    79
chartered psychologists, 15
chemistry, 2, 112, 117
Chomsky, N., 95
Christensen, L., 148
Clark, K.E., 4
client- (or person-) centred
    therapy, 30–31, 51
codes of conduct, 140–142
    changes in, 142
(*see also* British Psychological
    Society, and American
    Psychological Association),
coercion (of psychiatric patients),
    167
cognition, 3, 7
cognitive
    approach, 1
    behaviourism, 20
    development, 7
    (*see also* Piaget),
    developmental approach, 102
    learning, 7
    processes, **4**, 7
        attention, 7
        concept-formation, 7
        and free will, 39
        language, 7, 20
        memory, 7, 13, 20, 58, 77
        perception, 7
        problem-solving, 7
        reasoning, 7
        thinking, 7
    psychology, 4, 102, 103

revolution, 4, **94**-95
science, 4
Cohen, J., 28
Cold War, 68
Collins, H., 99, 105
Colman, A.M., 146
Committee of the Experimental
    Psychological Society, 140,
    158
computer
    analogy, **4**, 94, 103
    assisted learning (CAL), 20
    science, 3
Comte, A., 87
conditioning 2, 19–20, 24, 103,
(*see also* behaviourism),
    and advertising, 73,
    and associative learning, 19
    and the behaviour therapist's
        dilemma, 50–51
    classical (Pavlovian or
        respondent), 18–19, 50, 73,
        94, 97,
    and imagery, 19–20
    and learning, 2
    (learning) theory, 7, 104
    operant (instrumental), 19, 48,
        49, 50, 97, 169
    and the illusion of free will,
        49, 169
    and S–R psychology, 19, 103
confidentiality, 140, 148,
    150–151, 165
conformity, 9
    experiments (Asch), 110, 147,
        156
conscious mental life (CML), 46
consciousness, 54, 58, 90
    stream of (James), 91

consent, 140, 143–145, 151, 152, 165, 168
  presumptive, 156
  prior general, 156–157
constructionist explanations of behaviour, 55
context-stripping (and objectivity), 95
convergent thinking (and IQ tests), 83
Coolican, H., 10, 11, 13, 16, 80, 81, 145, 151
cost–benefit analysis
  in non-human experimentation, **162**
  in social psychology, **156**
  (*see also* double-obligation dilemma)
Cowie, H., 102
Crawford, M., 118
Crick, F., 56
criterion-referenced assessment (in IQ tests), **81**
cross-cultural psychology, 128–135
  advantages of, 134–135
  and ethnocentrism, **128**–130
  goals of, 128
  and national cultures, 130–131
  and problem of equivalence, **134**
Cullen, C., 165
cults, 64, 67
culture, 130–134
  definitions of, **130**
  and the emic–etic distinction, 132–134
  objective aspects of, 130
  subjective aspects of, 130

cultural
  bias (*see* ethnocentrism, and Anglocentric bias)
  differences, 131
  syndromes, 131–132
    cultural complexity, **131**
    individualism–collectivism, **131–132**, 135
    tight vs. loose, **132**
Dallos, R., 165
Darley, J.M., 154
Darwin, C., 92
Data Protection Act (UK), 150
Davison, G., 102, 167, 168
Dawkins, M.S., 158, 164
debriefing, 140, 146, 147, 148, **149**–50, 155
  therapeutic, 149–150
deception, 140, 144, 146–148, 151, 154, 156
  in Milgram's experiments, 144
  justification of, 147–148
  and self-image, 146
  stooges (confederates) in, 139, 146
  and subliminal advertising, 76
Deci, E.L., 41
Deese, J., 99, 112
Defence Research Board (Canada), 67
deficit model (of minority group performance), 134
dehoax (*see* debriefing)
Delgado, J.M.R., 40
demand characteristics, **108**–109
  and experimental control, 112
Denmark, F., 125–126, 128
Descartes, R., 43, 55, 87, 88
determinism, **38**, 39

hard, **46**
psychic, 46–48
soft, 39, **45**–46, 52
development,
  atypical, 9
  lifespan approach in, 8
  moral, 122
diminished responsibility, 42, 44
dispositional attributions, 135
divergent thinking (and IQ tests),
  82
DNA molecule, 56
doctrine of informed consent, 51
dopamine, 53
double obligation dilemma (of
  social psychologists), **155**–7,
  possible solutions to, 156–157
Drakeley, R., 79, 80
dream interpretation, 22
(*see also* psychoanalysis),
*Diagnostic and Statistical Manual
  of Mental Disorders (DSM-II)*,
  123
*Diagnostic and Statistical Manual
  of Mental Disorders (DSM-III-
  R)*, 123, 124
Dunsdon, M.I., 68
Eagly, A.H., 120
ego
  defence (*see* repression)
  psychology, **24**
Eiser, J.R., 59
electrical self-stimulation of the
  brain (ES-SB), 160
Elliot, C.D., 81
Ellis, A., 26
emergent properties (of the
  brain), 58
emic–etic distinction, 132–134

emics, **133**
empirical, **89**
empiricism, **89**
empirism, **88**, 89, 94
endocrine (hormonal) system, 6
epigenetic chart (Erikson), 127
ergonomics (*see* engineering
  psychology)
Erikson, E.H., 22, 24–25, 104,
  126, 127
(*see also* psychodynamic
  approach),
Eros, 67
ethical
  guidelines, 140–142
  (*see also* British Psychological
    Society, and American
    Psychological Association),
  ethics of, 152–153
  need for, 142–143
  imperative (Brehm), 154
ethics
  of advertising, 75–76
  and the aims of psychology, 154
  and appropriateness, 139
  of behaviour change, 64–65,
    164–170
  and human betterment, 154
  and methodology, 153, 157
  of Milgram's obedience
    experiments, 144–147
  of the prison simulation
    experiment, 144–147
  of psychological research with
    humans, 142–157
  of research with non-humans,
    158–164
  and socially meaningful
    research, 154–156

ethnocentrism, 110, 117,
128–130, 133
(see also cross-cultural
psychology),
ethological theory (Lorenz), 68
etics, **133**
imposed, **133**
eugenicists, **122**
Eurocentric bias (see Anglocentric
bias)
evolution of adult consciousness
(Gould's theory of), 24
eyewitness testimony, 7
exchange theory (of relationships),
135
executive monkey experiments,
158–159, 160
The Exorcist, 74
experimental control, 111–113
and extraneous variables,
111–112
participant, 112
situational, 112
experimental realism (see internal
validity)
experimenter bias, **107**–108
and children's IQ, 108
and experimental control, 112
and rats' performance in mazes,
107
and self-fulfilling prophecy, 108
experiments with non-humans,
158–164
justification of, 160, 162–164
safeguards in, 160–162
scientific value of, 162–163
and suffering, 158–159
Eysenck, H.J., 24, 26, 27, 67
Eysenck, M.W., 95

Fairbairn, G., 165, 166
Fairbairn, R., 25
Fairbairn, S., 165, 167
false memory syndrome, 13
Fancher, R.E., 25, 26, 27, 49, 89,
90, 92, 93
F(Fascism)-scale, 77
feminism, 118
feminist psychology, **117**–128,
142, 154
and criticisms of psychology,
118–119
and criticisms of psychology
experiments, 120
and critique of science,
119–121
and ethics, 142, 154
and male power, 118
and mental disorders, 123–124
and values, 119–121, 154
field studies, 10
Flanagan, O.J., 45, 56
Fode, K.L., 107
freedom
and anxiety reduction, 168–169
and behavioural control,
168–169
and power, 169
and the token economy, 169
free association, 22
(see also psychoanalysis),
free will, 20, 56
definitions of, 37–51
and determinism, 37–52, 165
and diminished responsibility,
42, 44
and divided attention, 41–42
and the humanistic approach,
28, 32

as an illusion, 46, 48, 50, 169
and intrinsic motivation, **41**
and moral accountability,
44–45
in psychological abnormality,
43–44
and psychological reactance, **40**
in psychological theories,
45–52
and Tourette's disorder, 37–38
and voluntary behaviour, 40,
54
Freud, Anna, 24, 25, 68
Freud, Sigmund, 3, 12, 20,
22–27, 28, 31, 32, 45,
46–48, 51, 53, 59, 63, 67,
68, 73, 92, 104, 128
fully functioning person (Rogers),
52
functionalism, **92**
fundamental attribution error,
134
Gale, A., 140, 142, 144
Gardner, H., 83
Garnham, A., 53
Garonzik, R., 110, 148
Garrett, R., 18, 21, 48, 50
Gay, P., 47
Gelder, M., 44
gender bias (*see* androcentic bias)
general problem solver (GPS), 95
genetic transmission, 7
Gestalt (school of psychology), **3**
laws/principles of perception, 3
psychologists, 29
therapy (Perls), 26
Geuter, U., 67
Gibson, J.J., 66
Giddens, A., 120

Gilligan, C., 122, 127
Glassman, W.E., 21, 29, 103
Gould, R.L., 24,
Gould, S.J., 66, 121, 122, 124
Gray, J.A., 160, 161, 164
Green, S., 162, 163
Greenwald, A.G., 75
Gregory, R.L., 54
Gross, R., 7, 11, 56, 67, 97, 103,
119, 134, 169
Grosz, E.A., 128
hard determinism (*see*
determinism)
Harré, R., 58, 95
Hartley, J., 10, 11
Hartnett, O., 119, 121
Hawks, D., 170
Haworth, G., 159
Hayes, N., 73
Heather, N., 106, 111
Hebb, D.O., 67
heredity and environment
(nature–nurture) issue, 7
hermeneutic strength (of Freudian
theory), **27**
Herrnstein, R.J., 152
Herskovits, M.J., 130
heterosexism, **119**
heterosexuality, 119
hierarchy of needs (Maslow), 28,
29
Hilliard, A.G., 152
Hitler, Adolf, 66, 71
Holmes, D.S., 38
Holmes, J., 25, 170
Holocaust, 122
Home Office (HO) Inspectors
(and animal experiments),
161

Homicide Act (1957), 44
Horney, K., 29
Howe, M., 153
Howitt, D., 153
humanistic approach, 1, 28–32
    and phenomenology, **28**, 55
    practical contributions of,
        30–31
    principles and assumptions of,
        28–30
    theoretical contributions of,
        29–30
Hume, D., 88
hypothetical constructs, **77**
id, 29
identity
    vs. role confusion (Erikson),
        127
    and the mind–brain relationship
        contingent, **56**
        token, **58**
        type, **58**
Immigration-Restriction Act
    (U.S.A.), 121–122
imposed etic, 133
individual psychology (Adler), 25
individualism (as a form of
    explanation), **118**, 119, 120,
    124
    vs. collectivism, 132
indoctrination, 64, 67, 76
industrial relations (*see*
    occupational psychology)
infantile secxuality (Freud's theory
    of), 23
information-processing approach,
    94, 102, 103
(*see also* cognitive approach, and
    cognitive revolution),

information processors (people
    as), 4
informed consent (*see* consent)
Institute of Medical Ethics (ME)
    Working Party, 159
intelligence, 58, 77,
    artificial, 95
    as an imposed etic, 134
    social, 82–83
intelligence (IQ) tests, 13, 77, 134
    arguments for and against,
        81–83
    bias in, 83
    and discrimination, 121–122,
        152–153
    individual, 81
        army alpha and beta, 122
        British Ability Scales (BAS),
            81
        Stanford–Binet, 121
    and self-fulfilling prophecy, **83**
interpersonal perception, 7, **9**
interpretation of resistance, 23
(*see also* psychoanalysis),
intimacy vs. isolation (Erikson),
    127
introspection, 1, 2, 16, 90
introversion–extroversion
    (Eysenck), 67
invasion of privacy, 145, 147
Israeli, R., 68
Jacobs, M., 22, 26
Jacobson, L., 108
Jahoda, G., 128
James, W., 2, 3, 39, 45–46, 89,
    91–92, 94
Jensen, A., 152
Joynson, R.B., 103
Judas Priest, 74

Jung, C.G., 22, 25
Kaufman, S.R., 163
Keane, M.J., 95
Kelley, H.H., 135
Klein, M., 25
Kline, P., 27, 28, 102, 103
Koestler, A., 42
Kohlberg, L., 126, 127, 128
Korean War, 67
Krupat, E., 110, 148
Kuhn, T.S., 99, 102, 106
Ladd, G.W., 69
Lambie, J., 104
Latane, B., 154
law of parsimony (Occam's razor), **19**
Lawson, R., 107
lay therapy, 31
leadership, 9
learning, 7, 8, 9
    associative, 19
    (*see also* conditioning),
    cognitive, 7
    insight, 7
    observational (modelling), 7
    programmed, 20
    theory, 7
    (*see also* conditioning)
LeFrancois, G.R., 103
Legge, D., 6
Leippe, M., 74, 75, 76
Lepper, M.R., 41
Levinson, D.J., 126
lifespan approach (in developmental psychology), 8, 24
Little Albert (case of), 97
localisation of brain function, **6**
Locke, John, 19, 88, 94

logical theory machine (logic theorist), 95
Lorenz, K., 68
Luria, A.R., 52
mainstream psychology, 1, 16, 24, 95–96, 109, 110, 117, 152
    and scientism, **95**–96
Mapstone, E., 158
masculinist bias (*see* androcentric bias)
Maslow, A., 28–29
masochistic personality (and women), 123–124
Masson, J., 169, 170
maze-bright rats, 107
maze-dull rats, 107
McIlveen, R., 7, 11, 97, 119, 169
McNaughton Rules (1843), 44
mechanism, **87**–88, 111
Medawar, P.B., 99, 100
medical justification (argument for non-human experimentation), 160, 162–164
    and speciesism, 164
mental
    disorders (*see* abnormal psychology)
    maps (Tolman), 7
    measurement (*see* psychometric tests)
    processes (*see* cognitive processes)
Mental Health Act (1983), 44
Milgram, N.A., 68
Milgram, R.N., 68
Milgram, S., 66, 144, 145, 146, 147, 148, 149, 150, 156, 157
Miller, G.A., 4, 94, 95

Milner, P., 160
mind–body problem, 37, 54–59
mind–brain relationship (theories
    of), 55–58
  dualism, **54**, 55, 57
  epiphenomenology, **55**, 57
  interactionism, **55**
  materialism
    centralist (mind–brain identity
        theory), **55**–56, 57
    eliminative, 56, 57
    peripheralist, **55**, 57
  mentalism (idealism), **55**, 57
  monism, **55**, 57
  psychophysical parallelism, 55,
      57
Minnesota Multiphasic
    Personality Inventory, 78
Minsky, M., 95
modelling (*see* observational
    learning)
Moghaddam, F.M., 109, 129,
    130, 134, 135
The Moonies, 76
Morea, P., 50, 51, 52
Morelli, G., 135
Morrison, A.R., 163
motivation, 7,8
Mukerjee, M., 161, 162, 163
mundane realism (*see* external
    validity)
Murray, C., 152
Myers, D.G., 154
National Curriculum, 81
nativism (or rationalism), 88
Nazi propaganda, 71
Neale, J., 102, 167, 168
neurobiological (biogenic)
    approach, 1

neuroticism–stability (Eysenck),
    67
neutrality (of therapists), 168
Newell, A., 95
Newman, M., 69
Nicolson, P., 120, 121
nominal fallacy, **31**
nomothetic approach, **109**
norm-referenced assessment (in
    IQ tests), **81**
Norman, D.A., 41
obedience, 9
  experiments (Milgram), 66,
      144–148
  ethics of, 144–148
object realtions (British) school,
    25
occupational assessment (and
    personality tests), 79–80
Oedipus complex (Freud), 23, 25
Office of Naval Research (U.S.A.),
    67
Olds, J., 160
operational definitions, **19**
Orne, M.T., 108, 109, 139
overdetermination (Freud), **47**
Packard, V., 74
Palermo, D.S., 103
paradigm (as a criterion of
    science), **102**, 106
  vs. an approach, 104
paradox of reward, **41**
parapraxes ('Freudian slips'), **47**
Pavlov, I.P., 93
Penfield, W., 40
Penrose, R., 58
perception, 1, 3, 4, 7, 8
  Gestalt laws of, 3
  Gibson's theory of, 66

interpersonal, 7, 9
subliminal, 73–**74**
peripheralism
Skinner, 55
Watson, 53
Perls, F.S., 26
personality, 77
person approach, 6, 8–10
personnel management (see
occupational psychology)
persuasion, 63, 64
of psychiatric patients, 167
persuasive communication, 66
phallic stage (of psychosexual
development), 23
phallocentric (nature of Freud's
psychosexual theory), 128
phenomenal field (Rogers), **30**
philosophical
dualism, **54**, 55, 87
roots of psychology, 87–89
philosophy, 1
empiricist, 19, **88**, 94
nativist, **88**
physics, 2, 112, 117
micro, 53
revolution in, 103, 106
Piaget, J., 7, 8
Pietromonaco, P., 75
Pike, K.L., 133
Piliavin, I.M., 147
play therapy, 25
Popper, K., 26, 27, 99, 100, 101
positivism, **87**, 117, 152
positivist approach (of natural
science), 28, 28, 52, 87, 94,
96, 117
post-traumatic stress disorder
(PTSD), 66–67, 68

and Vietnam War veterans, 67
and World War II children, 68
Pratkanis, A., 69, 72, 75
presumptive consent, **156**
Prince, J., 119, 121
Prins, H., 44
prior general consent, **156**–157
prison simulation experiment, 67
problem of mind and brain (*see*
mind–body problem)
process approach, **6**–7, 9–10
programmed learning, 20
propaganda
vs. education, 72
as a form of persuasion, 64
and war, **69**–71
protection of participants, 140,
142–143, 148–149, 154
vs. benefiting society, 153–156
vs. harming the group, 151–153
psychiatrists, **12**, 43, 164, 168
forensic, 44
influence of, 168
psychiatry, 5, 44, 64, 65, 166
psychic determinism (Freud),
46–48
psychoanalysis, 3, 12, **22**–23, 47,
102, 166, 169
dream interpretation, 22
free association, 22, 47
interpretation of resistance, 23
transference, 22
psychoanalytic theory, 3, 20, 22,
28, 63, 128
psychodynamic approach, 3,
22–27, 29, 32, 104
practical contributions of, 26
principles and assumptions of,
22–23

theoretical contributions of, 24–25

psychologists
  as agents for change (practitioners), 11, 50, 139, 164–170
  chartered, **15**
  as colleagues, 10–11
  as counsellors, 10
  as detached investigators (scientists), 11, 139
  as experts, 11, 170
  responsibilities of, 122, 166
  as teachers, 170
  as technicians, 170
  as theoreticians, 11
  as toolmakers, 11

psychology
  abnormal, 9
  academic, 6, 10
  and advertising, 73–76
  aims of as a science, 19, 21, 93, 139, 154, 170
  analytical (Jung), 25
  applied, 6, 9, 10–15
  bias in, 117–135
  clinical, 9, 10, 11–12, 20, 64, 65, 164, 165
  controversial applications of, 63–84
  counselling, 11, 31
  criminological (forensic), 10, **12**–13
  cross-cultural, 128–130
  definitions of, 1–4
  developmental, **8**
  educational, 10, **13**–14, 164
  ego, 24
  empirism and, 89

engineering (or ergonomics), 14
environmental, 10
experiments, 106–113
  artificiality of, 111
  power differences in, 111
  as social situations, 106–109
  validity of, 111–113
feminist, 117–128
and government service, 10
health, 10
individual (Adler), 25
mainstream, 1, 16, 24, 95–96, 109, 110, 117, 123, 135
military, 67
as objective science, 11, 87–113
  and scientism, **95**–96
occupational (work, organisational), 10, **14**–15
propaganda and, 69–72
social, 7, 9
social influence and, 63–65
sociology and, 5, 120
sports, 10
as value-free science, 95–96, 165–166
  (*see also* positivism),
  war and, 65–69
    Wehrmacht (armed forces), 67

psychometric tests, 11, 12, 13, 76–83
  ability vs. attainment (achievement), **80**
  of aptitude, 14, 80–**81**
  discriminatory power of, 77
  of intelligence (IQ), 13, 63, 66, 67, 80–83
  of interest, 14
  of personality, 78–80

objective, **78**

projective, **78**

questionnaires and inventories, **78**

reliablity of, 77–78

standardisation of, 77, 78

uses of, 78–83

validity of, 77–78

psychosexual stages of development (Freud), 23, 53, 128

psychosocial stages of development (Erikson), 25

psychotherapists, **12**, 164

and abuse of patients, 169–170

influence of, 167–168

power of, 169–170

as psychological midwives, 167

as value neutral/non-directive, 165, 166–167

psychotherapy, 3, 12, 26, 64, 65

and behaviour therapy, 167–168

and ethics, 164–170

outcome studies of, 12

public health campaigns, 72

Q-sorts, **31**

Quicke, J., 81

Rampton (special hospital), 13

rational emotive therapy (RET), 26

reaction formation (and the unfalsifiability of Freudian theory), 26–27

recovered memory, 13

reductionism, 37, 52–59, 88

and anti-reductionism, 59

and the autonomy of psychological explanation, 59

and experimental control, 112

and levels of description/universes of discourse, 59

and the mind–body problem, 37, **54**–59

and voluntary behaviour, 40

reification, **77**, 121

reinforcement theory, 18

(*see also* conditioning),

representativeness (of participants), 109–111

research

applied, **6**

pure, **6**

Richards, A., 100

Richards, G., 65, 66, 67, 77, 104, 105, 152

Richardson, K., 105

right to withdraw (from an investigation), 140, 145, 148

Ringen, J., 50, 51

Rogers, C.R., 26, 28–31, 45, 51–52, 55

Rogoff, B., 135

Rose, S., 53, 58

Rosenthal, R., 107, 108

Rowan, A.N., 162

Rushton, J.P., 152

Ryan, R.M., 41

Rycroft, C., 48

Ryder, R., 164

sadism (and men), 124

Scheier, M.F., 41

schizophrenia, 53

science, 97–104

as a cultural phenomenon, **109**

feminist critique of, 119–121

major features of, 97, 98, 99

definable subject matter, **97**, 98

hypothesis testing, **97**, 98

theory construction, **97**, 98

use of empirical methods, **97**, 98

objectivity and, 105–109

as a social construct, 105

social nature of, 104–109

stages in the development of (Kuhn)

normal science (paradigmatic), 99, **102**, 103

pre-science (pre-paradigmatic), **102**, 103

revolution (paradigm shift), 99, **103**, 106

scientific justification (argument for non-human experimentation), 160

scientific method, 97, 99–**100**, 120

classical view (inductive method), 100, 101

hypothetico-deductive method, 101

and clinical psychology, 165

scientific racism, 122

scientism, **95**–96

scientist–practitioner model (of clinical psychology), **165**

Scodel, A., 26

self (Rogers), **30**, 51

self-actualisation (Maslow), 28, 29, 31, 51, 52

self-defeating personality disorder, 124

sensory deprivation, 67

sexism, 110, 117, 119

in research, 125–126

in theory, 127

Shallice, T., 41

Sherif, M., 135

Simon, H.A., 95

Skinner, B.F., 16, 18, 19, 20, 21, 28, 43, 45, 46, 48–51, 55, 97, 169

Skinner box, **21**

Smith, C.U.M., 56

Smith, J.A., 96

Smith, P.B., 128, 131, 132, 133, 135

Smith, P. K., 102

social learning theory, 7, 20

sociobiology, 102

soft determinism (*see* determinism)

spatial ability (and sexism), 126

speciesism, **164**

standard assessment tests (SATs), 81

Stanford–Binet (IQ test), 121

states of consciousness, 6

Sternberg, R. J., 83

stereotypes, 7

of mental illness, 166

in propaganda, 71

of scientists, 100

of women, 118, 119

Stevens, R., 27

Strachey, J., 46

stress, 7

structuralism, **1**, 53, 90, 103

(*see also* introspection, and Wundt),

Studer, C., 129, 135

Sue, S., 152

Sulloway, F.J., 46, 47

Sutcliffe, Peter (Yorkshire Ripper), 44

systematic desensitization, **26**

tabula rasa (blank slate), 94

Tavris, C., 123, 124

Taylor, R., 38

teaching machines, 20

technical illusions (Milgram), 147, 155

Teichman, J., 56

Thanatos, 67

theoretical approaches, 15–32
  behaviourist, 16–21
  humanistic, 28–32
  psychodynamic, 22–27

therapeutic debriefing (*see* debriefing)

therapist qualities, 31

Thibaut, J.W., 135

Thorndike's puzzle box, 21

Thorne, B., 30, 31, 52

thought reform, 64, 67

Tolman, E.C., 20

transactional analysis (Berne), 26

transference, 22
(*see also* psychoanalysis),

Triandis, H.C., 128, 130, 131, 132

Trower, P., 166

unconscious mind
  collective (or racial), 25
  personal, 25
  and repression, 22
  in young children, 25

unfalsifiability (of Freudian theory), **26**

Unger, R., 118

UNICEF, 69

U.S. War Department, 66

Valentine, E.R., 103, 107, 108

validity (of experiments), 111–113
  external (ecological), **111**, 112, 155
  internal, 111–112

Van Langenhove, L., 95, 96

variability (of human beings), 112

Vicary, Jim, 73, 74, 75

voluntary vs. involuntary behaviour, 40

Wachtel, P.L., 168, 169

Wadeley, A., 74

Watson, John B., 2–3, 16, 19, 53, 55, 73, 92–94, 97, 103

Wechsler, D., 81

Wechsler
  Adult Intelligence Scale (WAIS), 81
  Intelligence Scale for Children (WISC), 81

Weisstein, N., 108

Wertheimer, M., 29

Wilkinson, S., 117, 118, 125, 128

will to power (Adler), 25

Wilson, G., 125

Wilson, G.D., 24

Wilson, G.T., 31

Wober, M., 134

Wolpe, J., 26

Wolpert, L., 100

Wundt, Wilhelm, 1,2, 3, 89–90, 92, 94, 103

Yom Kippur War, 68

Zimbardo, P.G., 4, 67, 74, 75, 76, 144145, 149-150

Ziv, A., 68